NORTHERN REFLECTIONS

A lighthearted account of
"Growing Up North"

by Jerry Harju

NORTHERN REFLECTIONS

A light hearted account of "Growing Up North"

by Jerry Harju

Illustrations by
Craig MacIntosh

Copyright 1993
by Jerry Harju

Published by North Harbor Publishing
528 E. Arch St. Marquette, Michigan 49855
Toll Free (877) 906-3984
e-mail: jharju@bresnanlink.net

Publishing Coordination by
Globe Printing Inc. Ishpeming, Michigan

ISBN 0-9670205-1-4
Library of Congress Card No. 92-075914

First Edition - November 1992
Reprinted 1993, 1995, 1998, 2000

INTRODUCTION

I don't think I could hack it as a kid today. It's bad enough, right now, getting up in the morning and facing myself in the mirror. If I had to sport one of those 1990's teenage haircuts, I'd go into cardiac arrest in the bathroom.

And, how do you learn to dance to music that sounds like a train wreck? I had enough trouble learning the box step to get through The Blue Skirt Waltz.

I walked into a video arcade not too long ago and saw a ten-year-old kid at the controls of an F-15, expertly taking out Iraqi tanks with laser-guided missiles. I was twelve before I got real good on a two-wheel bicycle.

These days, kids in the sixth grade are writing programs on personal computers. I didn't learn how to operate a slide rule safely until I was eighteen.

Now a kid has to figure out how to get forty or fifty dollars to buy a pair of jeans with stylish torn-out knees. I used to get "that look" free of charge by tripping over the ties on the railroad tracks.

So, this book is a collection of circumstances that I considered big deals when I was growing up in Upper Michigan in the 1940's. If you're about my age, you can probably identify with some of them. If you're younger, you'll probably say to yourself: Why is he writing about dumb things like that? That's nothing compared to what kids have to go through today!

That's alright...if you wind up buying the book, I can live with that.

Jerry Harju
528 E. Arch St.
Marquette, MI 49855
Toll Free (877) 906-3984
e-mail: jharju@bresnanlink.net

DEDICATION

*To my mother and father, Lydia and Arvid Harju,
and my sister, Esther Greenwood.*

Books by Jerry Harju

Northern Reflections
Northern D'lights
Northern Passages
The Class of '57
Cold Cash

ACKNOWLEDGEMENTS

Every book represents a culmination of time and energies of many people other than the author. I thank my sweetheart, best friend, and editor, Pat Green, whose relentless red pen bloodied up my manuscripts. I also thank Chris, Mike, Cam, Loretta, Roger, and others who stroked my ego by telling me that the stuff wasn't too bad and then let me know what was wrong with it. Finally, I want to thank Anita McCollum at Avery Color Studios, whose encouragement allowed me to see this book as a reality.

The L.S.& I. Meets a Superhero

*T*he panes in my bedroom window started to hum, then shifted to a busy vibration, and finally intensified to a rattling climax, as the first iron-ore train of the day passed within forty feet of where I lay comfortably in bed. I listened to the ore cars click over the spacing between the rails. This was a short one; he was going pretty fast. If the train had more than a hundred ore cars, the engineer had to slow it down to a crawl to get up the slight grade by our house, on his way to the Marquette loading docks. I looked over at the big brass alarm clock on the wooden dresser. Quarter to eight. Yup, he was right on time.

Usually, the first ore train was the signal for me to get up and get ready for school, but today...today was a red-letter day! The first day of summer vacation! It was mid June of 1940, and last Friday I had successfully escaped from the first grade. Miss Barbosa, our first-grade teacher, would have to sharpen her ruler on someone else's knuckles next year! Without opening my eyes, I smiled and burrowed my head further down into the pillow. It was going to be a great summer! The only thing that troubled me was that my mother had told me that I had eleven more years of school left to go. Would I live that long? My old man had only made it through the sixth grade, and look how old he was!

"Hey, Jer!...Jer...you up yet?"

I pushed up the lower pane of the window and looked down at Kippy Hanson, my pal who lived on the other side of the railroad tracks. He looked up at me from beneath the bill of a baseball cap, which was two sizes too big. His mother believed in planning ahead.

"Jeez...you still in bed? C'mon, it's vacation! I got sumthin' t'show ya!"

"Whadizzit?"

"I ain't gonna tell ya. Ya gotta see it. C'mon down!"

I got into my oldest corduroys, which were my usual vacation pants, and went down to the kitchen. My mother was frantically running bed sheets through the wringer of our Maytag washer. When you lived this close to the railroad tracks, wash-day was a real exercise in planning and timing. It had to be sunny, and you had to get the wash out on the clothesline right after the first ore train went by, so it would be dry and taken down before the second train came. Otherwise, the wet wash got peppered with soot from the steam locomotive. I was only seven, but I knew from experience that you didn't get in Ma's way when she was doing the wash.

Without saying a word, she stopped the wringer, went over to the stove, and filled a bowl with oatmeal. She put it down with a thump on the oilcloth on the kitchen table and went back to the washing machine.

"Aww, Ma, it's summer! It's too hot fer oatmeal. Kin I have some Wheaties?" Jack Armstrong was hawking his latest decoder ring on his five-thirty radio program, and I needed three Wheaties box tops. I had even tried to get the old man interested in Wheaties the other morning, but he just gave me a peculiar look and kept dunking his Rusk toast in his coffee cup.

My mother gave me her patented, petrifying stare that she used when she was going to lay down the law about something.

"The oatmeal's made, an' the Wheaties'll keep till tomorrow. But, do you know what that oatmeal'll look like tomorrow morning if I make you eat it then?"

I sighed and poured cream into the oatmeal. My dog, Teddy, got up from the rag rug that he had been lying on, and came over and put his muzzle on my thigh. That dog really had the life. He didn't have to go to school or eat oatmeal.

I went through Kippy's back door into his kitchen, where he was eating a bowl of Wheaties. Jeez! Was he going to get the decoder ring before me? I wish I could move over to his house! He reached over to the corner of the table and quickly palmed something.

"Hey! What'cha got?"

Slowly, he opened up his hand to reveal a shiny copper disk about the size of a quarter. It had a man's head on it.

"Whatizzit?"

"It's a penny!"

"Iz not! It's too big!"

"I put it on the rail, an' the first ore train mashed it."

I picked it up. It was a penny all right. But, why would anybody want to do that? You probably couldn't spend it now, and a penny would get you six malted-milk balls or three licorice sticks down at Niemi's store. Maybe my mother was right when she said that Lutherans had more sense about money than Methodists.

I gave him the penny back. "Why'ja do that? It's no good now!"

Kippy gave me a crafty leer and lowered his voice. "I hadda try it on a penny first, but I gotta way to get rich! You wanna get in on it?"

"Whaddaya mean?"

He got up from the table and, standing on a chair, got a Mason jar down from one of the kitchen cupboards. He poured out a pile of coins onto the table and fished out a nickel and a quarter. He put them side by side.

"Here's what'cha do. You put a nickel on the rail, an' when the train flattens it, it'll look jus' like a quarter. See? Washington and Jefferson are even looking in the same direction! Ol' man Niemi can't see very good anyhow, and we kin take it down to his store an' get all the ice cream we want!"

I looked at the coins on the table. "I dunno...Jefferson's hair looks different."

"Wait'll the train takes care of 'im. He'll look a lot more like Washington then."

It was a pretty good idea, but a nickel was a big investment. "Whose money is this?" I said, pointing at the coins on the table.

"My mother's milk money."

"So...you gotta nickel?"

"My ol' man iz gonna gimme one tonight."

The next day Kippy, Teddy, and I were standing at the soda fountain in Niemi's store. The hand holding the huge vanilla ice-cream cone shook, and I stared down at the floor to keep from making eye contact while Kippy paid for the two cones with "the coin." The only one of us who wasn't scared was Teddy, who was expressing doggy outrage at not getting a cone. Old man Niemi looked down at what Kippy had put in his palm.

"What iz this? D'you think yer the first kids t'come in here with nickels that you've flattened with the ore train an' try to pass 'em off as quarters?" He pointed at the dripping vanilla cones that Kippy and I held in our hands. "You better have a dime fer those cones!"

Kippy looked around uneasily. "That's the only money we got."

"Then the ice cream comes back!" Niemi grabbed Kippy's arm to get the cone, but the sudden jerking motion dislodged the huge scoop of vanilla loose from the cone, and it sailed up in the air.

Teddy, who was sitting on the floor behind us, leaped high, and deftly snatched the ice-cream ball in mid air with his jaws. With one distinct, gulping sound, it was gone. My teeth ached just watching it. Teddy sat back on the floor and looked at me, waiting for the other scoop to drop. I quickly handed the cone back to Niemi, and we all ran out of the store. Old man Niemi came out from behind the counter, shaking his fist.

"I don't wanna see you kids in this store again until you have a nickel to pay fer that cone!"

So much for our road to riches.

The summer droned into July, and Kippy and I continued to pass the time by flattening different things on the rails. Nails were the favorites because they were plentiful and did a nice job of getting flat. Two nails laid in an X pattern made a really nice cross, suitable for wearing around the neck—we had a fleeting notion of making them in quantity and selling them to the French and Italian kids, who were big on that sort of thing. But, any kind of dialogue with them usually ended up in an iron-ore fight, so we dropped the idea. One hot afternoon I went over to Kippy's house and plunked a railroad spike into his hand.

"So, whattaya goin' to do with this?"

I smiled. "You think the train can flatten it?"

"I dunno. We ain't tried anything that big before."

"If it got flat, it'd make a really great point for a spear!"

Visions of getting a big edge on the French and Italian kids went through Kippy's mind. "Yeah! Let's try it!"

The last ore train of the day came chuffing up the slight grade about four o'clock. We put the spike on one of the rails and stood in my front yard to see what would happen. The wheel behind the cowcatcher hit the spike with a shower of sparks, bounced over the spike with a loud THUMP!!!, and knocked it off the rail. The engineer had been sitting in the locomotive cab window, with his elbow resting on the sill and his chin in the palm of his hand—probably thinking about supper. The bounce and THUMP!!! brought him back to his senses, and he looked around wildly. Then, he spotted the two of us standing there and guessed what had happened. He shook his fist and started yelling at us. The train was making too much noise for us to hear what he said. It was probably better that way. Kippy and I both went in for supper without checking the spike. We knew we had gone too far.

About seven o'clock that night there was a knock at our kitchen door. My mother opened it to see a stranger standing there, hat in hand, nervously working over the brim with his fingers.

"Hello, missus. You don't know me, but my name is Emil Erikson, an' I live in Negaunee. I work for the Lake Superior and Ishpeming Railroad."

My mother gave him a blank stare, and he pointed off to the left at the rail-road tracks.

"You know...the L.S.&I. trains that run by here every day."

My mother nodded. He continued.

"Well, I'm one of the engineers, an' your kids have been puttin' things on the rails to flatten them, like kids do...but this afternoon they put somethin' on the rail that made the engine jump. Now, I gotta tell ya, I wasn't payin' real close attention, so I don't know what it was, but if they put anythin' like that on the tracks again, you may have the locomotive right here in your kitchen. You don't want that, do you?"

My mother gave me a poisonous glare. "Only one of those kids belongs to me, but I'll take care of it."

The engineer left, and my mother slammed the door. She reached over and grabbed me by the hair, hoisting me up until only the tips of my shoes were touching the floor. Our noses almost touched.

"So...only seven years old an' you've decided to take up wrecking trains..."

It was a rainy afternoon in late August. Kippy and I were sitting in his kitchen, reading comic books, and having our favorite afternoon snack of catsup sandwiches. I think catsup sandwiches were invented by the Methodists during the Great Depression, but my mother flatly refused to recognize them as real food, so I had to go over to Kippy's house to get them.

We both had gotten a sound whacking for the railroad spike incident, so we had to turn our attention to other things. One of our latest passions was comic books.

Comic books were new in the Upper Peninsula, but they had taken hold like a forest fire. Every kid had become intimately familiar with the exploits of Superman, Captain Marvel, Batman and Robin, Captain America, and the like. The price of ten cents a copy made it too expensive for everybody to buy the latest monthly edition of their favorites, so there was a lot of trading of used comic books. The appetite for fresh reading material had gotten so great that Kippy and I had temporarily declared a cease-fire with some of the French and Italian kids this morning to pull off a big trade.

All day long I had been wrestling with the dilemma of whether or not I ought to let Kippy in on a secret. But, what good was a secret if you were the only one who knew about it? I finally put down the August edition of *Captain America* and gave him a solemn look.

"If I let you in on a secret, will you promise not to tell anybody?"

"Sure."

"Promise on your mother's grave?"

Kippy blinked his eyes. "My mother ain't dead."

"I know, but that's what you say when it's a big secret."

"OK. I promise, on my mother's grave, not to tell."

"Well...I decided that I'm gonna be a crime fighter."

"You mean you wanna be a cop?"

"No...no...whadda cops know? I mean like Captain America."

Kippy crinkled his eyes and grinned. "Hah! Fat chance! You see the muscles on Captain America? Those crooks'd tie you in knots!"

"Yeah, but if I start now I kin be jus' like that when I grow up!"

"Start now? Where you gonna start? There ain't any crime around here! All those guys like Superman, Batman, Captain America...they live in big cities like Green Bay and Milwaukee! When's the las' time you seen bank robbers and murderers here in this town?"

"Well...guys like that prob'ly started on smaller things when they wuz kids..."

Kippy stared at me in disbelief. "When they wuz kids? They ain't real! Some a them are bulletproof! When's the las' time you seen a bulletproof guy aroun' here? Some a them fly! You seen anybody fly around here lately?"

"The Green Lantern ain't bulletproof, an' he don't fly!"

"If you got shot as many times as the Green Lantern does, you'd be in the hospital the res' a your life!"

I was getting mad, and I stood up. "That don't mean there ain't guys like that around!"

"My ol' man reads *The Daily Mining Journal* every night, an' he ain't said anything about crime fighters!"

I leaned over, looked him in the eye, and said in a whisper, "Then maybe I might be the first one!"

Kippy thought about that awhile. "So...whaddaya gonna do now?"

"That's what I been thinkin' about. I figure that you gotta start off by doin' somethin' courageous."

Kippy narrowed his eyes. "Whaddaya gonna do?"

I leaned over and stared into his eyes. "I'm gonna stop the ore train."

Kippy jumped back like he had been bitten. "Stop the ore train??? You're crazy! You can't stop the ore train! My ol' man sez he don't think that even the engineer can stop the ore train here once he's got it goin' from the mine. He's gotta start slowin' it down in Negaunee jus' t'stop it in Marquette!"

"He kin stop it all right. He's goin' uphill when he goes by here. An' lemme tell ya somethin' else. I'm gonna stop ol' Emil Erikson's train. I ain't forgot he squealed on us when we put the railroad spike on the track."

"How ya gonna get Emil Erikson t'stop the train?"

"I'm gonna stand on the tracks."

"Stand on the tracks? He'll come over yer house again an' tell yer Ma, an' this time she'll kill you fer sure! That's courageous all right! Nice knowin' ya!"

I gave him my slyest grin. "He ain't gonna know it's me on the tracks."

"Why not?"

"That's the second part a my secret. I got another identity."

"What?"

"I'm Victory Boy!"

"Yer what?"

"C'mon over to my house, an' I'll show ya my other identity."

I left Kippy sitting on the bed in my room, carried a paper bag into my parents' bedroom, and closed the door. On their chenille bedspread, I carefully laid out the pieces of my new identity. The colors of my Victory Boy uniform were red and white. This was good because it didn't match with any of the other superheroes that I knew. First, the trousers would consist of white leggings with red trunks. I was lucky there because I was able to cut a pair of my last winter's long underwear in half and use the bottoms. They were pretty tight because I had outgrown them, but the last thing you wanted in a superhero costume was baggy leggings. Over those, I would put my old red swim trunks, which looked really snappy. It also solved the problem of how to hide the trap door of the underwear bottoms, even though a trap door might come in handy after a particularly intense courageous act. Then, there was the long, bright-red woolen stockings, which used to be part of my winter snowsuit. Going to be a little warm in the summer, but I couldn't lay my hands on red boots, so they'd have to do. The upper half was a white T-shirt which had gotten shrunk in the wash and fit like a sausage skin, but this was good because you wanted your muscles to show through. But the grandest part of all was the red V that was sewn on the chest.

The name Victory Boy had come to me in a blinding flash, one night three weeks ago, when the old man had taken us to the Butler Theatre to see the latest Marx Brothers movie. Suffering through the newsreel, I noticed a fat guy on the screen in a derby hat, coming out of a house on a narrow street, holding two fingers in the air.

"What's he doing that for?" I whispered.

The old man leaned over. "That's Churchill, an' the fingers mean "V for Victory." He's tryin' to egg the English into beatin' the Nazis."

V for Victory!!! That was it! Every time I'd grab a crook, I'd hold up those two fingers with my free hand!

Not only did it have a nice ring to it, but a V was easy to cut out and sew on the shirt. I had to do it myself to keep my new identity a secret. My mother gave me a real suspicious look when I asked her for sewing lessons, but she couldn't see any possible connection between sewing and derailing L.S.&I. locomotives, so she taught me the basics of needle and thread.

Finally, to hide my identity while I was in action, I had come up with a particularly ingenious idea. I had filched a gauzy red scarf from one of my mother's drawers, and by putting it across my face and tying all four corners in a knot on the back of my head, it made a perfect face mask. It gave everything I saw a fuzzy red hue, but my vision was easily good enough for what I had to do.

I got into my Victory Boy costume and walked into my bedroom. Kippy stared in admiration.

"Wow! That's neat! But, it don't have any eye holes. You might trip over a railroad tie."

"Naw...I kin see fine."

"When you gonna stop the train?"

"Tomorrow afternoon."

The next afternoon, everything was working out fine. The old man was out at the potato farm, my older sister was gallivanting around someplace with her friends, and my mother was doing the grocery shopping. I had the house to myself, perfect to change into my other identity.

At quarter to four, I got into my Victory Boy garb and waited on the bed in my room. At five minutes to four, I heard the steam whistle blow at the Division Street crossing and knew that it was only a matter of minutes before the train got to our house. I jumped up and ran downstairs. My first test of courage was only moments away.

Teddy was lying on his rug in the kitchen and got up with a quizzical look when he saw me.

"An' whose dog are you?" I said, in my best Lone Ranger voice.

He wagged his tail and jumped up on me with his front paws, snagging my V with one of his doggie claws.

"Get down! Get down! I got work to do!" I went out the kitchen door with Teddy on my heels. He sensed that something out of the ordinary was about to happen—maybe another errant, vanilla ice-cream cone.

I got up on the tracks just as the smoke from the locomotive was visible in the west. In a matter of seconds, the train came into view about a quarter mile away. A moment later the steam whistle shrieked. He never blew the whistle after the Division Street crossing! That means he's seen me! This is working out great!

The rails started to hum, and the whistle blew again. Teddy had followed me onto the tracks, but now he looked at the oncoming train and began to whine. He

. . .to hide my identity. . .I had come up with a particularly ingenious idea. . .

looked at me, hung his head, and started backing off the tracks. The dog obviously had no stomach for courageous acts. I was thinking about making him my sidekick, but who wants a sidekick that whines?

Any second now Emil'll start jamming on the brakes, I thought, but all I heard was the whistle scream a third time.

I saw something out of the corner of my eye, off to my left. I looked over and saw Kippy standing in his yard, yelling, and pointing behind me. But the train was making too much noise, and I couldn't make it out.

And then I was airborne! Jeez!...did I get hit by the train? My head was really hurting. No...the train was still quite a way off, but I was moving off the track, and my feet weren't touching the ground! Did I somehow get superhero magical powers? My body slowly turned around, and then I saw her. My mother had come up behind me, lifted me up by the hair, and was carrying me down to the house. She wound up with her free hand, and I felt intense pain as she smacked me across the butt. My body turned with the force of the blow, and I caught a glimpse of the locomotive as it passed. Emil Erikson was grinning and clapping his hands!

After his debut on the railroad tracks, Victory Boy retired from the superhero business, and in a few months my mother had finally started speaking to me in complete sentences again. Around the beginning of December she had even asked me what I wanted for Christmas! So, things had pretty much gotten back to normal by Christmas day. I was sitting at the kitchen table, eating a thick slab of homemade saffron bread covered with Philadelphia Cream Cheese—two things that were available in our house only at Christmas.

There was a knock at the kitchen door. My mother opened it, and Emil Erikson was standing there. The saffron bread fell from my fingers, and the cream cheese side hit the table.

He had on a suit and necktie underneath his mackinaw, and his hair was plastered down with Wildroot Creme Oil. "Hello missus, I don' know if you remember me. I'm Emil Erikson, the engineer who works for the L.S.&I. I was here last summer, remember?"

My mother's head whipped around and she looked at me, baring her upper plate in a snarl.

"I didn't do nuthin', Ma! I ain't even been on the tracks since las' summer!"

Emil quickly put up his hand. "No...no...yer kid ain't done nuthin'. It's jus' that after I seen you carry him off the tracks las' summer and spankin' 'im good, I got to feelin' sorry fer the li'l guy. He really mus' like trains to be foolin' around the tracks alla time like that. Anyway, this year, the L.S.&I. gave us a real good Christmas bonus, an' I brought somethin' around to make it up to him." He reached down at his side and lifted up a bulky cardboard box and brought it in and put it on the kitchen floor.

It was an electric train.

My mother's hand flew up to her mouth. "Oh, my gosh!" The old man had come in from the living room and was staring at it unbelievingly. I had never even dreamed of getting an electric train!

Emil went to the door. "Maybe he'll take an interest in this train an' stay away from mine! Merry Christmas and Happy New Year!" He laughed and opened the door to leave. My mother pinched me savagely on the arm, and I quickly thanked him. The old man had already dragged the train into the living room.

What was I going to do now? All of that planning! All of the preparation! Now I couldn't go through with it!

Ever since the first good snowfall after Thanksgiving, Kippy and I had hatched a plan so brilliant—so crafty—so sure-fire—so evil in purpose, that we surprised even ourselves. We had struck an alliance with the French and Italian kids and had built a snow fort next to the railroad tracks down at the Frenchtown siding. We then laboriously stocked it with a formidable supply of "ore-balls." An ore-ball was made by forming a snowball around a chunk of iron ore. Then you poured water over it, letting it freeze into a hard shell. The older Frenchtown kids assured us that if an ore-ball was made properly, it could put a dent in a locomotive boiler, and most certainly remove an ear from the engineer's head.

You see, what we had in mind was to ambush Emil Erikson when he made his four o'clock run next Monday. The most insidious part of the plan was that Kippy and I would have our woolen scarves across our faces, and Emil would assume that it was the Frenchtown kids who were to blame. It was a beautiful plan, and now I couldn't go through with it! Emil had given me an electric train! Why did he have to turn out to be such a nice guy? What was I going to tell the gang?

The old man had taken the train out of the box and was now avidly reading the directions out loud about operating the transformer.

I pretended to be interested, but who would want to play with a toy train when you had just outgrown playing with the real thing, right outside your door?

The old man picked up the toy locomotive and the lights from the Christmas tree gleamed off his eyeballs, "Ya know, I think I know where I can lay my hands on a piece a plywood that would hold all a this track..."

The Revenge of the 'Rithmetic Wizard

*T*he old man picked up one of his checkers and jumped three of mine to reach my back row. "King me!" he barked.

Gawd! How did I miss that? I was getting that hot lump in my throat again, as I was in immediate danger of adding yet another to my losing streak of about three thousand straight games. I could have rationalized it by the fact that this was a monumental day in my life, and that I wasn't concentrating. But, who was I kidding? The old man was the undisputed checkers champion of our neighborhood. Anyone who came over to visit suddenly remembered urgent appointments whenever he dragged out the checkerboard. So, I was frequently drafted into a game in order that he could hone his skill.

My parents and I were sitting in the railroad depot in Ishpeming, Michigan, in the Upper Peninsula, waiting for the train to take us to Milwaukee. It was early November, 1942, and World War II was in full swing. While everybody expressed shock and horror at the daily exploits of Tojo and Hitler, there was no denying that it had charged up the humdrum existence of the whole country. Even I had been caught up in it. I was religiously saving my pennies for Defense Stamps, and the walls of my bedroom had been covered with maps of Europe and the Pacific and silhouettes of enemy aircraft. If the Germans had sent in a squadron of Focke Wulf 190's to strafe the Upper Peninsula, I would have spotted them in an instant.

But my life was about to take a more pivotal turn. The old man had suddenly announced that we were moving to Milwaukee for the duration of the war. The wartime jobs were too enticing to pass up with sky-high wages in the two-dollar per hour range. I had never been out of Marquette County, and Milwaukee sounded as remote as the Emerald City in the Land of Oz.

"Yer not concentratin' on yer game!" he said, as he wiped me out again.

13

My mother looked up from the task of rearranging the thirty-six meat loaf sandwiches, wrapped in waxed paper, in the A&P shopping bag that she was going to take on the train. A good supply of meat loaf sandwiches could get you to the far reaches of the solar system.

"Why don't you let him win a game once in awhile?"

"He'll win when he gets good enough," he replied. The old man figured that losing was part of building one's character.

I hated checkers more than I hated the Nazis.

"Class, I want you to meet Gerald, who has moved from the Upper Peninsula of Michigan to join us at Kilbourn Grade School, here in Milwaukee. Gerald, would you please stand up?" The teacher turned and beamed at me.

I stood up from behind a desk in the back of the classroom and confronted a sea of curious and hostile fifth-grade faces. My right leg buckled slightly and my palms were clammy. The last time that I felt like this was when I had to recite the Twenty-Third Psalm from memory in front of the Lutheran congregation at the age of six. I managed a sickly smile and hurriedly sat down.

At recess I quickly got the "new kid" treatment in the schoolyard. I was immediately surrounded by a welcoming committee of five surly-looking fifth-grade thugs. The leader, a narrow-eyed kid with muddy-colored hair and a chipped front tooth, stuck his face in mine and gave the opening address.

"Well, Gerrruuuld...so yer from the Upppperrrrr Peninnnsulaaaa! An' jus' where izzat?"

I gave him my best Gary Cooper expression. "North of here."

"Oh? Up by Green Bay?"

"Much further north. It took the train four hours just to get down to Green Bay."

His squinty eyes widened a bit. "Yer really from the sticks! See many bears up there?"

I saw my opening and went for it. "Heck yeah! Alla time! One a them is so tame that I feed him right outta my hand."

"Polar bears?" one of the other kids asked.

I thought about that for a second but decided not to press my luck. "No, just black bears."

The head thug wasn't buying it. "I don't believe this crap!"

But I had set him up perfectly. My uncle Arvid, who made it through the Great Depression trapping mink and muskrat, lived in a cabin outside of town. One morning he had taken a picture of a bear outside of his door and given it to me. I fished the picture out of my wallet and stuck it three inches from his eyes.

"Jeeeezzz! OK...but where are you?"

"Who d'ya think took the picture?"

I instantly became a member in good standing of the Kilbourn Street Gremlins.

I leaned across my desk and whispered to the girl sitting in front of me, "What's she doing?"

The teacher was chalking up a random assortment of addition, subtraction, multiplication, and division problems in a horizontal line across the wide blackboard.

"She's setting up the arithmetic bee."

"What's an arithmetic bee?"

"A kid starts on each end of the board and works the problems, going toward each other. The one who gets the most problems right wins the match."

"Then what?"

"Then she puts up a new set of problems, and two more kids get up there and do it. She keeps doing it till there are only two kids left, and then they go at it to see who's the champion."

"Kind of like a spelling bee with numbers, huh?"

"Yeah, I guess so."

I looked at the first set of arithmetic problems on the blackboard. They looked pretty simple to me. This was stuff that had been drummed into me in the third and fourth grade. I may have been from the sticks, but the Upper Peninsula's educational standards were as brutal as its winters. Reading, writing and arithmetic were dealt out in relentless quantities and the incentive to learn was dirt simple: pay attention, or experience real pain.

My mind drifted back to fond recollections of some of my earlier academic struggles. Miss Barbosa, our first grade teacher, no doubt a direct descendant of the Spanish Grand Inquisitor, had a novel teaching technique: while patrolling the room during penmanship class, if she didn't like your Palmer Method ovals, she would rap the offending hand with her ruler. The ovals became doubly challenging as your fingers went numb. Brigette O'Reilly, our third grade teacher, blessed with legendary upper-body strength, would pick up a malcontent by his hair and carry him over to the supply closet where he would be locked up for an indefinite sentence. Mutt Hakala, one of my classmates who had a particularly mulish attitude about mastering eight's and nine's, developed a real taste for library paste during his many hours of solitary confinement in the supply closet. Since I had a low threshold for pain, I decided that learning was the easiest way out.

The teacher snapped my reverie by rapping on her desk.

"OK, class, we're going to begin this week's arithmetic bee..."

I leaned across my desk again. "This looks pretty easy, huh?"

The girl in front of me whispered out of side of her mouth. "It doesn't make any difference. The same girl wins it every time. You don't stand a chance."

I watched the preliminary rounds until my name was called. There were fifteen problems across the board. I was pitted against some faceless fat kid—I demolished him eleven to four. Some time later I was matched up with a girl who was a bit quicker, but I brushed her aside nine to six.

The afternoon droned on; the air became heavy with chalk dust and the perspiration of the slow-witted. The teacher made the problems harder as we marched through the quarter-finals and into the semi-finals, but I defeated two more opponents with little difficulty. I wasn't paying close attention to every match, but I started to notice a leggy brunette girl with long curls that came down to her waist. She was knocking off her opposition with practiced ease, and I figured she must be the one that I heard about from the girl sitting in front of me. The tougher problems weren't slowing her down, and she humiliated some kid with thick glasses to reach the finals. I took on a red-haired girl who choked up when she dropped her chalk on the floor, and that's all it took. I beat her ten to five in the last semi-final match.

The teacher got up from her desk and took my hand at the blackboard.

"Class, we've now reached the final match, and I'm very pleased to see that our new student from the Upper Peninsula has done so well. He must have studied his arithmetic very hard to be this good."

You bet I had...the alternatives hadn't been pleasant to think about.

The teacher held out her other hand.

"Janice, I want you to come up here and meet Gerald." The brunette with the curls came up and joined the teacher and me at the blackboard.

"Gerald, Janice has been the arithmetic bee winner for many weeks now, so you have a tough opponent."

While the teacher was putting the last problem set on the board, I turned and got my first good look at the brunette at close range. She was, without a doubt, the most beautiful girl that I had ever seen. She had large dark eyes surrounded by lashes that were longer and thicker than the hair on my head. Our eyes locked, and she flashed a sultry thousand-megawatt smile at me. My body temperature shot up ten degrees, and my face started to burn up. Was that how she did it? She would just give a budding young mathematician that smile, and he'd permanently forget his multiplication tables and be doomed to a life as a short order cook.

"Janice and Gerald, we're now ready to start. Good luck to you both!"

I closed my eyes momentarily to get that smile out of my brain. If I had looked at her a second longer, I would have been a goner. But I picked up my chalk and set out on the task at hand.

Chalk squeaked furiously as we both attacked the problems from opposite ends of the blackboard. A quick glance to the right told me that she was keeping up with me, problem for problem. We got to our seventh problem at the same time with the final problem left between us. Her seventh problem was twenty-eight times thirty-nine, and she hesitated a split second while carrying the seven. That was all the edge that I needed, and I got to do the last problem to win the match eight to seven.

The room erupted with yells, whistles, and applause. It was an upset of momentous proportions. The teacher came up and, with a wide smile on her face, grabbed me by the shoulders.

"Well! Congratulations to you, Gerald! It looks as if we now have a new arithmetic wizard!"

The brunette came up to me, flashed that smile, and stuck out her hand.

"de Marco"

"What?"

"The teacher didn't tell you my last name. It's de Marco."

For a second, I had forgotten mine, but I recovered and introduced myself. She gave me one last smile and went to her seat.

After school was out, my fellow Gremlins came up to me in the schoolyard. The leader, whom I now knew as Murph, punched me on the shoulder.

"Hey, 'rithmetic wizard! Boy, was I glad to see ya give it to her! She always hasta be the best at everything. She's so stuck up she never talks to anybody in the class. Not even the girls! I heard the teacher tell her once that she had a high IQ, whatever that is. If she's got a high one, then I want a low one. Right?"

"That's right!" one of his disciples cried.

"We'll make it a Gremlin slogan. LOW IQ! LOW IQ! LOW IQ!"

We stood there and chanted our new battle cry for a minute or so. Several teachers leaving the building looked at us in astonishment, no doubt unnerved by our solidarity. I was caught up in the esprit de corps of my new friends as I walked home to our two-bedroom apartment that my parents had rented last week. My first day at the new school had been an unqualified success. I had achieved a status that I had never dreamt possible. Life in the big city was going to be a breeze.

"You're very good at arithmetic."

I whirled around and there she was, walking up behind me. My Captain Midnight lunch bucket clattered to the sidewalk.

"Uhhh...thanks. You're pretty good yourself."

She was every bit as tall as I was, a physical limitation that I would have to endure until the ninth grade. She fixed those huge black-brown eyes on mine, like a lioness sizing up an antelope.

"Where do you live?"

"On Eighteenth Street, near Wisconsin Avenue."

"Oh? That's close to our apartment on Seventeenth Street."

I was quickly running out of pleasantries. "Uh...that's nice."

"Would you like to come over to my place for lunch on Saturday? We could play some games."

"Uh...I dunno. I'm pretty busy right now." I didn't like where this was going at all. I had never played games with a girl, except for Alice Maki, who had an incredible right arm, and helped me and my pals fend off the French and Italian kids with chunks of iron ore from the railroad tracks.

"We live on the twelfth floor in that tall building on the corner. You can see the lake from our window."

"You live on the twelfth floor?" I couldn't believe what I was hearing. Ever since we had hit town I had been obsessed with the tall buildings, trying to figure out a way to get to the top of one. Back home, the tallest structures around were three-story buildings or housings for mine shafts.

"Yeah. That does sound like fun. What time shall I come over?"

"Is noon OK? My parents will be working, so it'll just be the two of us."

She gave that high-voltage smile again. For a few seconds, I forgot where we lived.

I was excavating a wing rib out of a sheet of balsa wood from a Boeing B-17 bomber model airplane kit when the old man came home. He was working on an assembly line at International Harvester, putting Army trucks together for the princely sum of $2.15 an hour, so we could afford the very best in model airplanes.

"So how was school today? You didn't get whacked, did you?"

"I don't think the teacher whacks kids. She smiles a lot, an' is pretty nice."

He puckered his brow. "Don't whack anybody? What kinda school is that?"

My mother came in the door. She had a job a few blocks away making brassieres for the Women's Army Corps.

"So how was school today?"

The old man turned to her. "He sez that the teachers don't whack anybody. Sounds like he got it pretty soft t'me."

"Well, the city kids are probably nicer than that rough gang up north."

I put down my Exacto knife. "Hey, I won the 'rithmetic bee today, an' the girl I beat invited me over to lunch next Saturday. She lives on the twelfth floor!"

My academic accomplishment was lost on the old man. "Ya mean t'tell me that you been in school one day, an' you got a date with a girl? I dunno who you take after!"

"It's not a date, Pop. We're jus' goin' to have some lunch an' play some games."

"What's her name?" my mother wanted to know.

"Janice de Marco."

"de Marco? That sounds Catholic. Does she go to church?"

"I dunno. I didn't ask her."

The old man winked at me. "This is the big city. He can go out with a Catholic girl here an' no one'll ever find out about it."

My mother sighed. "Well, OK. When we go to that Lutheran church on Twentieth Street next Sunday, maybe you might see some girls there from your class."

"I am not going out with this girl, an' I don't want to look for Lutheran girls in church! We're jus' goin' to play some games next Saturday!"

The old man gave me a thin smile. "Play some games... Well, when you get a little older that'll take on a whole new meaning."

The next morning, before the bell rang, I had joined the Gremlins in the schoolyard and let it slip about my "date" on Saturday.

Murph's eyes narrowed to slits. "Are you kiddin' me? She jus' came up to you an' invited you over to lunch while her parents are workin'? Ya know what? She's got the hots for you!"

"Hots?"

He gave me a conspiratorial grin. "I'll bet if you play your cards right you can get in."

"Get in?" I found out later that Murph was the Gremlins' resident expert on sexual education, a prerequisite for the head Gremlin job.

"Yeah! You know what 'get in' is doncha?"

"A course I do!"

"Now that I think about it, she goes for brainy guys. We had a kid in our class last year that knew all the capitals of the forty-eight states, an she started givin him that crazy smile. But, he moved out of town. Since you're the new 'rithmetic wizard, I'll bet you're in like Errol Flynn!"

Anxiety started to nibble at my brain. I had two passions in life: building model airplanes and identifying enemy aircraft. While I had my share of crushes on cute girls, it was a short-lived, detached pastime which didn't require any decision-making or out-going behavior. But this rendezvous with the girl on 17th Street was taking on a murky dimension with ground rules that were never explained to me. If she's got the "hots" for me, should I act "hot"? If so, how is it done? Should I try to "get in"? "Get in" what? When? How? I now knew one thing for sure. I should have blown one or two of those problems on the arithmetic bee final. Life was sure simpler with only model planes and enemy aircraft.

Saturday arrived as a gray, blustery, and cold day. I thought about calling off the lunch several times, but the twelfth floor kept beckoning to me. Finally, I decided on the strategy of going over there, looking out the window, wolfing down whatever there was to eat, and going home before things got weird.

My mother had made a point of checking out the building where the de Marcos lived and had immediately decided that this was strictly a "put on the dog" operation. It was the tallest and most elegant building in the neighborhood. I had been forced into a premature haircut, and now she was laying out my church-going attire on my bed, like a matador's suit of lights.

"What are you going to have to eat?"

"I don't know, Mom. I didn't ask her."

"Well, make sure you use a napkin, if she's got them on the table, and don't eat too fast."

I put on my new suit that we had bought at the Boston Store last week. My mother spotted an errant price tag on the waistband and cut it loose with my Exacto knife. I made a mental note to get back to the Boston Store and ride the escalator some more. We knotted my necktie three times, but the narrow end still came out longer than the wide end. I headed for the door, putting on my mackinaw.

"And don't chew with your mouth open!"

I surveyed the revolving door carefully. I had already logged in some time on them at the department stores downtown, but I'd seen plenty of movies where unpleasant things can happen to people who got careless with revolving doors. I delicately inserted myself in the door and made it into the Wisconsin Arms Apartments.

The lobby had a subdued atmosphere with a plush gray carpet that extended all the way to the wall in every direction. The only person in sight was a man in a brown uniform sitting in a chair next to the far wall. He was tapping a cigarette in a heavy, bronze, floor-model ashtray.

"Lookin' for someone, young fella?"

"Uh...yeah. Janice de Marco. She lives in apartment 1201."

"Well, that's on the twelfth floor."

"Yeah, I know. Uh...where's the stairs?"

He looked at me closely for several seconds and butted out the cigarette in the ashtray. He got up from the chair and opened a door with a glass window in it. It was an elevator.

"Why don't you let me give you a ride up there?"

Of course! An elevator! How could I be so dumb! Any building this tall would have an elevator in it.

I had never ridden in an elevator.

"Come on, step inside."

I walked into the small compartment and stood there facing the far wall.

"You can turn around if you want to."

He closed the door and turned a crank mounted on a circular brass plate on the elevator wall. We started to move up. I closed my eyes.

"You're not from around here, are you?"

"Uh...we moved here last week."

"Well, welcome to the big city!"

He opened the elevator door, and I stepped into a deserted hallway which stretched off in two directions. I could see windows at both ends of the hallway. I ran down to one of the windows and pressed my nose against the glass. What a view! Gawd! She was right! You could see Lake Michigan off on the horizon.

I looked to my left at the apartment door. It was marked 1201. I knocked on the large wooden door. The door was so thick that it felt as if I was bashing my knuckles on a slab of granite. I got no response after several knocks, but then discovered the doorbell. The door gave off a muted click and opened with a whispering against a thick carpet inside of the apartment. I was looking into those huge black-brown eyes.

"Hello. You're right on time."

"Uh...that's right! I'm never late for a meal. Heh, heh, heh."

She was wearing an light-blue Angora sweater with a matching pleated skirt, topped off with a wide silk ribbon in her long black hair. I could feel another fugitive price tag on the inside of my waistband burrowing into the small of my back.

"Well, don't just stand there. Come on in!"

My J.C. Penney shoes submerged into the deep pile as I stepped into the biggest living room I had ever seen in my life. It was something out of a Fred Astaire-Ginger Rogers movie set.

"Wow! This is about twice as big as our classroom! It must cost a pile a money to rent this!"

"Would you like me to show you around?"

But I was already at the window which faced uptown. "Hey! Look! You wanna see where I live on Eighteenth Street?"

She walked over to the window.

I pointed down and to the left. "See that apartment house with the green roof? It's got some missing shingles. You can't see my bedroom window, though. It's on the other side."

She feigned interest. "Oh, yes. I see it now."

"You mind if I open the window?"

"Oh...my father told me to never op..."

"Jus' for a minute." I undid the latch and jerked up the lower pane. An ugly, frigid blast of air, fresh from Lake Michigan, assaulted the apartment.

I stuck my head out and looked down. "Wow! Look! The cars look like bugs crawling around!"

"Uh...it's getting pretty cold in here."

"Oh...yeah." I closed the window. "What a neat place to fly model airplanes from! Have you ever flown a model out of one of these windows? I bet with the right wind it would go right down to the lake!"

"No...I've never built a model."

"No? Well, I guess girls don't build 'em. I'm workin' on a Boeing B-17 right now. You know those big four-engine jobs? Each engine's got its own prop with a rubber band. I gotta figure out how to keep three of the props wound while I wind up the fourth. It's got a bunch a neat decals, even with little swastikas that you paste under the cockpit to show how many Nazi planes that the gunners have shot down!"

So far everything was going great. I hadn't realized that it would be so easy to talk with girls.

"Here, I'll show you the rest of the apartment."

"OK...Jeeeeeez!!!!!!... What's that?" I pointed at a bizarre montage hanging in a prominent position on the living room wall.

"Oh, that's a Picasso that my mother bought last year."

"What's a Picasso?"

"Picasso's a famous artist. He gets a lot of money for his paintings."

"Oh, yeah? I thought maybe it was something that you drew when you were in kindergarten. My mom used to hang up pictures that I drew when I was a small kid."

She giggled. "No, silly. It's supposed to look like that. My mother says it's surrealistic."

"Sure realistic? It don't look real at all... What's that in the corner of it?"

"Uh...I think it's a dog."

"A dog? Well, one of his eyeballs is really in the wrong place! Though...I did see a dog that looked sumthin' like that, excep' he had been squashed by an ore train. Well, if this guy's so famous, this must'a cost a lot."

"No, not really. This is just a print."

"A print?"

"It's not the real painting. It's just a copy."

"A copy! Boy, yer mom must'a been mad when she found that out! I hope she didn't get gypped too bad."

She giggled again. "She knew it was a print when she bought it. It only cost fifteen dollars with the frame."

"Fifteen dollars? An' it's not even the real thing!" I let out a low whistle. "Yer folks must have good jobs!"

"My father is an engineer, and my mother is a curator at the museum."

"An engineer! I knew it! They mus' make a lotta money! Does he drive a steam locomotive or a diesel?"

This time I really cracked her up. I was definitely getting the knack of entertaining girls.

"Not that kind of engineer. He figures out how things should be built."

"Kind of like a carpenter, huh?"

"Well...I suppose so. Shall we have lunch now?"

"Yeah! Boy! I could eat a horse! What're we havin' to eat? I mean...uh...I kin eat anything, but my mother wanted to know."

"My mother made us some shrimp cocktails and turkey sandwiches."

"Cocktails? I better not. My old man'd kill me if he found out I'd been drinking cocktails, no matter how small they were."

This time she laughed out loud. "You mean you've never had a shrimp cocktail? It's seafood."

The only thing that I had eaten that lived in water was trout, perch, walleyed pike, and smelt. When the old man felt really extravagant, he would invest in a couple of tins of kippered herring.

"Well, I'll try anything. Bring it on!"

I followed her into a kitchen that was twice the size of the living room in our apartment. A gigantic white refrigerator quietly hummed in the corner. There were no dirty coffee cups in the sink or paper bags full of garbage. A shiny toaster sat on the counter, notably devoid of crumbs. Everything else was out of sight. I sat down at the kitchen table.

"No. Don't sit there. We'll have lunch in the dining area."

I followed her out of a different door from the kitchen into an area with a massive, dark, wooden table with six ornately carved chairs. Two places were set with twelve-inch plates, small forks, and neatly folded white napkins.

"Sit down here, and I'll bring in the food."

She went back into the kitchen, and I sat down and studied the place setting. I remembered what my mother had said about the napkin, so I grabbed it and tried to stuff a corner into the collar of my shirt. But my mother had cinched the necktie up good. I unbuttoned the collar, loosened the tie, and inserted the napkin. No one could say that I didn't have table manners.

She made three trips from the kitchen, bringing in tall glasses of milk, turkey sandwiches on separate plates, and...the infamous shrimp cocktails. She put the shrimp cocktail on the large plate in front of me.

"This is the shrimp cocktail?"

"Yes. You eat them with the small fork."

"Uh...don't get mad, but they look like skinned caterpillars."

She put down her fork and glared at me. "They do not! Try one. They're good!" She speared one and dipped it into a metal dish sitting between us.

"You dunk it in the catsup to kill the taste?"

"It's shrimp cocktail sauce."

"Well, here goes." I closed my eyes and swallowed one. Not bad! There were only about eight of them in my dish, and I polished them off in about a minute. I picked up one half of the turkey sandwich.

"How come there ain't any crust on the bread?"

"My mother cuts it off when she makes sandwiches."

"Yeah? Boy! If I asked my mom to do that, she'd think I'd gone crazy."

I bolted the sandwich and washed it down with half a glass of milk. She gave me an amused smile. "You've got a milk mustache."

I delicately wiped off my upper lip with the sleeve of my suit coat.

She cleared off the table, putting the dirty dishes in the sink for some elves to spirit off. She came back in to the table.

"You want to play a game?"

I stifled a belch. "Sure. What games have you got?"

She gave me another one of those seductive smiles. I could feel my face heating up.

"We...llll. What I really want to do is..."

Oh-oh. Here it comes. Now I'm going to find out about "hots" and everything else that Murph was talking about. I wasn't ready for this! I started to nibble on my lower lip.

"...play chess!!!"

Chess??? Is that another name for "hots"? Is it anything like playing doctor? Do we keep our clothes on?

"What I really want to do...is play chess.

She put a wooden box on the dining room table. "My father and I have been playing chess for several months now. He said that if I ever found anyone at school who was really good at arithmetic, they'd probably make a good chess player. I really like to play a lot!" She emptied the contents of the box onto the tablecloth and turned the box over.

I recoiled in fright. "That's a checkerboard!"

"That's right. But it's also a chessboard." She started to put pieces of various shapes and sizes on the squares.

I broke out in a cold sweat. I could have steeled myself for a little sex education, but even the sight of a checkerboard brought on an anxiety attack. She didn't have the hots for me! She thought that I was going to be good at playing some stupid game on a checkerboard! This was turning into a very bad day.

Janice had finished arranging all of the pieces on the board. "It sounds like you haven't played chess before, but I'll explain the rules to you."

I got up from the chair. "Uh...I don't think so. I really don't care much for checkers and..."

She looked up quickly. "But this isn't anything like checkers! How do you know you won't like it if you don't try it?" She gave me a slow smile. "You liked the shrimp, didn't you?"

So I sat back down, and for the next half hour she gave me a cram course on the mysteries of chess. Since I was the 'rithmetic wizard, I opted not to write anything down, and my brain was starting to heat up by the time we started the first game.

My opening strategy was to wage a war of attrition on her pawns. I was piling up an impressive body count, thinking that this game wasn't all that hard, when one of her castles shot the length of the board to take out one of my castles.

"Leaving that rook open like that wasn't very good because..."

"Oh yeah? Well, I'll jus' stomp that rook with my horse and..."

"You can't do that. Remember that the knight can only move in an L shape."

Five moves later I was checkmated.

And so it went. In an hour I lost four games. Pieces leaped astounding distances from all directions to ambush me. When I was totally convinced that she was making up the rules as she went along, I got up from the table and started to put on my mackinaw. "It's been a lot of fun, but I really have to put together that B-17..."

She looked a little disappointed as she walked me to the door. "I know it's hard when you first start playing chess. My father says that it takes a long time to really become good at it. But, he says that if you start when you're a kid, you stand a much better chance of being a really good player than if you start when you're a grownup."

I paused with one arm hanging in the mackinaw. "You mean, like, if I really learned how to play now, that I could be better than my father, even if I taught him the rules?"

"Has he ever played chess?"

"I don't think he's ever heard of chess."

"Oh...I'm sure that you could beat him."

I detected the faint knock of the opportunity of revenge at the door of my consciousness. Taking the mackinaw off, I said "Maybe just a few more games. But, go over the rules again real slow. An' Janice, if your parents let you drink coffee, why don't you make a pot?"

Three hours later I had just won my first game when her mother came in the door. "Oh, Janice, I see that your friend from school is a chess player."

"Mother, this is Jerry. He's never played chess before, and he just beat me!"

I gave her mother a modest smile as I stood up and shook her hand. "Well, Janice beat me a lotta games before this one, but I'm really gonna like chess."

"Well, you know what they say, don't you? If you start playing when you're a youngster, you can beat adults in no time!"

I gave her an innocent smile. "Yeah, that's what I hear... Uh...how long do you think it takes to be a real good chess player?"

"Well, I don't want to discourage you, but a lot of people who know the game say that it takes about thirty years to really become accomplished at it."

I put my mackinaw on. "I better get going or my folks are goin' to wonder what happened to me...Janice, do you think that I could borrow the chess set? I can give it back to you Monday morning."

"Of course!"

Her mother beamed at me. "I'm so glad that Janice has found someone to challenge her. I really think she's far ahead of the other students in the class."

I walked to the door with the chess set under my arm. "Yeah, I know what you mean. Oh...Mrs. de Marco, I really like the Picasso. It looks like the real thing."

The elevator operator was nowhere in sight, so I walked down the twelve flights. But my mind was on other things as I walked down the stairs.

Thirty years...let's see...he's forty-seven now. In thirty years he'll be seventy-seven. I heard my mother say that the memory really starts to go bad after sixty. If there ever was a game that requires a good memory, it's chess! HE'LL NEVER MAKE IT!!!!! HE'S ALREADY TOO OLD TO BEAT ME!!!!

I could see the beads of sweat popping out on the old man's forehead and the nervous drumming of his fingers on the tabletop as he surveyed his hopeless situation on the board. I'd lean back in my chair and pull out my pocket watch. "You're only supposed to take a certain amount of time to make your move, Pop. I told you that during the last game."

No mercy. I'd show him no mercy at all. After all...losing builds character.

Headpin Hovi and the Lapland Curse

*J*ake Hovi's huge hairy hands dwarfed the bowling ball that he held up close to his nose as he took aim at the pins. He galloped awkwardly forward and, when only two steps away from the foul line, he suddenly swung the ball back in a vicious arc. At the top of his backswing, the ball was directly over his head. He fired it out toward the pins with all the muscle his two hundred and eighty pounds could muster.

POP!!!!.................CLUNK!!!!.....CCRRAAACCKK!!!

His thumb had exploded out of the ball a split second later than it should have, and the ball became airborne. My gawd, I thought, this time he's going to do it! The bowling ball's going to hit the pins on the fly! But, about ten feet from the pins, it landed on the alley with a thunderous CLUNK! and took out the four, seven, and eight pins. Jake had only been bowling for a week, so he wasn't very accurate, but he was going at it with a vengeance.

Stubby La Croix looked up from his cash register with a pained expression. "Gawdammit Jake! Take it easy on the alleys! I jus' had 'em varnished two weeks ago!"

Jake took a long pull on a bottle of Stroh's, gave Stubby an unconcerned stare, and belched as he waited for his ball to come back. "If you had balls with decent-size finger holes, that wouldn't happen!"

Stubby took a Lucky Strike out of the pack in his vest pocket and tapped it on the counter. He was the only guy in town who wore a vest on occasions other than weddings and funerals, but it suited his image. He was short, had graying wavy hair, and always sported a host of pens and pencils for doing quick calculations. Stubby had a long history of starting up businesses of various types around Marquette County, most of which ended up as financial equivalents of the ill-fated *Titanic*.

But, this time might be a different story. Stubby had just opened a four-lane bowling alley in our town, and everybody wanted in on the action. Up to now, locals who already bowled had to drive to Ishpeming or Marquette to do it, but the new bowling alley had also aroused the interest of townspeople who had never held a bowling ball in their life. There was something about drinking beer and throwing a large, heavy object that appealed to guys who made a living in the iron mines or out in the woods. I could see a glint in Stubby's eyes. He figured on being a rich man in a short time.

He lit the Lucky and gave me an appraising stare. I had just asked him for a job setting pins.

"Yeah, I suppose I kin give you a try on settin' pins. It pays six cents a game."

"Six cents! You're payin' Mutt Hukala eight cents a game!"

"Yeah, but Mutt's been settin' pins for a week now, an' he's pretty fast. You never done it before, an' you'll probably be slow as hell. Six cents. Take it or leave it! There's plenty a kids ready to take the job for six cents a game."

He had me there. A lot of the kids at school were talking about getting a job setting pins at the new bowling alley. It was 1946, and postwar prices of everything essential to my thirteen-year-old comfort were skyrocketing.

I gulped. "OK. I'll take it."

Stubby gave me a smug smile. "Awright. Go down to the pits, an' Mutt'll show you the ropes."

I walked down a passageway next to Lane Number One and through a door at the far end of the building. "The pits" were in a narrow room that ran the width of the bowling alley and housed the four pinsetting machines. Automatic pinsetters were still years away, and these machines needed someone to pick up the fallen bowling pins out of the pit behind the alley, put them into the machine, and set them back up on the alley again.

Mutt Hukala was setting pins on Lane Three for Jake Hovi. The only way to get from one pinsetting machine to another was a two-foot-wide wooden walkway behind the machines. The walkway was about three-and-a-half feet off the floor and also served as a bench for the kids who were setting pins. You hopped up and sat on the walkway while the bowler was throwing the ball. I jumped up on the walkway and went over to the Lane Three pit.

Mutt picked up the bowling ball from the bottom of the pit and put it on the ball return. He was stripped to the waist and bathed in sweat. He had a big black smudge on his stomach from holding the bowling ball against his body. He wiped sweat from his forehead and glanced up at me while he threw pins in the machine.

"Ya get the job?"

"Yeah...but he'll only gimme six cents a game."

"I ain't surprised. Every kid in town wants to set pins, but believe me...it ain't no picnic! You earn every cent!"

He grabbed a horizontal bar on the machine and pushed down on it, lowering the machine to the alley surface. The machine pushed the pins into an upright position and dropped them neatly on the end of the alley into their triangular formation. Mutt checked the pins to make sure that none of them were leaning on the machine, and then pushed the lever up to raise the machine. He then put the palms of his hands on the walkway and boosted himself up.

There was a thin wall coming down from the ceiling between the pinsetting machines and the bowlers, but it had slats in it, so the kids setting pins could see what the bowler was doing. Jake galloped into his approach and let fly with the ball.

POP!!!.................CLUNK!!!...CCRRAAASSHH!!!!!!!

This time Jake got it more in the center of the alley, and back in the Lane Three pit all hell broke loose! Pins were flying in all directions. Most of them crashed into the padding underneath the walkway, but one flew up and caught Mutt in the forearm and another one barely missed my ankle.

"Jesussss! You do this fer eight cents a game?"

Mutt hopped down into the pit and picked up the ball. "Aww...most a the time it's not so bad. It's jus' when guys like Hovi think they kin blow the pins over with fastballs that it gets a li'l excitin'."

I sat down on the walkway, and Mutt explained the finer points of setting pins. He showed me how to pick up two pins with each hand to save time, and how to jiggle the machine after it had dropped the pins on the alley, so that none of the pins were leaning on the machine when you got ready to raise it. The first thing you did was send the ball back to the bowler so you could pick up the pins while the ball was travelling along the return. Anything you could do to save time meant that the games would go quicker and you made money faster.

Within a week, I was a grizzled veteran employee of Stubby's bowling alley. I had been setting pins every night and had the badges of honor to prove it. I had splinters in my fingers from picking up cracked pins, since Stubby wasn't anxious to replace the expensive maple pins until they actually broke in half. My shins had been barked from flying pins until I got enough sense not to dangle my legs over the edge of the walkway when the ball came down. The trick was to swing your legs out toward the machine when the ball hit the pins. But when you were setting pins for

Jake Hovi, the only thing you could do was to pull your legs up on the walkway, cover the family jewels, and pray. It was hard, hot, and dirty work for coolie wages, and the enthusiasm for doing it quickly evaporated among the kids at school. In fact, Stubby had to raise my wages to eight cents a game to keep my interest up.

But Stubby wasn't short of customers. Every night the place was packed with bowlers and kibitzers. The air was thick with cigarette smoke, beer fumes, and free advice. People who had never held a bowling ball in their life wouldn't hesitate to tell you how to get a sharper hook on your ball or the best place to stand on the approach when you were trying to pick up a five-ten split. Stubby had put in several dozen used theater seats for the kibitzers, and even then, it was usually standing room only.

On Saturday night the joint was jumping as usual, and I was setting pins on Lane Two. Stubby was really short of pinsetters that night, and Mutt had brought in his younger brother, Kenny, to show him the ropes. Mutt was setting them up on Lane Four, and Kenny was working between us on Lane Three.

Kenny Hukala was only eleven years old, wore thick glasses, and wasn't what you would call really well-coordinated. He was too small to push down the machine with authority and also hadn't yet mastered the trick of jiggling the machine to make sure that each pin was standing up by itself before pulling the machine up. As a result, he'd hoist the machine and a pin would topple over, usually taking a couple more with it. Kenny then had to jump back down in the pit, reach out onto the alley, and set the pins on their spots by hand. This really slowed down the game, but everybody on Lane Three was having fun and nobody complained.

Then, at eight o'clock, Jake Hovi started bowling on Lane Three.

On the third frame it happened again. Kenny hoisted the machine, and the three pin fell over and knocked down the six and ten pins. Kenny jumped off the walkway quickly, got down there, and set them up by hand. A couple of Jake's buddies laughed, but Jake had been standing on the approach waiting to throw the ball when it happened. He slammed the ball back down on the ball return and walked to the foul line.

"Fer crissake kid! Didn' anybody show ya how t'set pins?"

After Kenny set the pins up by hand, Jake threw his ball, hit the head pin dead on, and got what you usually get when you hit the head pin on the nose. A split. As a matter of fact, the granddaddy of them all—a seven-ten split—so wide that you could drive a Jeep between the pins. Jake turned beet red, whipped his head around, and glared at Stubby.

"Stubby, get a kid down there who knows how t'set pins!"

"Ain't got any other kids tonight, Jake."

"I want somebody down there who knows what the hell they're doin'!"

Down in the pits Mutt got up on the walkway and walked over to Kenny's lane.

"Change alleys with me. That Hovi's a mean sunavabitch. I'll set fer 'im."

But Kenny had his share of the Hukala stubbornness. "Go 'way! I'll be OK! I'm gettin' the hang of it!"

Things settled down for a couple of frames, but then in the sixth frame, disaster struck. Jake was standing on the approach, ball in hand, waiting for Kenny to raise the machine. The machine went up, but the head pin hadn't been standing up straight and fell over when the machine cleared the pins. It fell into the two pin, which knocked over the five pin, which knocked down the nine and ten pins. Pins were rolling around all over the alley. I stopped what I was doing, waiting for Jake's reaction.

Kenny jumped into the pit and crawled out onto the alley, scooping up the fallen pins. Jake didn't say a word, but deliberately went into his approach and whipped the ball down the alley.

I couldn't believe what I was seeing! Kenny was almost flat on his stomach on the alley, gathering up pins, and the bowling ball was coming down at him about ninety miles an hour! Mutt sprang up onto the walkway.

"KENNY! GET OUTTA THERE!"

Kenny saw the ball coming, dropped the pins he had in his hands, and started to scuttle backwards off the alley. But, he wasn't nearly fast enough. The ball smashed into the fallen and standing pins, and Kenny was buried under an avalanche of flying wood.

Mutt and I both jumped into the pit of Lane Three. Kenny was lying there among the pins and Jake's bowling ball, his face covered with blood. One of the pins must have hit his glasses because the left lens was all smashed, and I couldn't see his left eye for the blood. He was also bleeding pretty good from the nose. Mutt took charge as he bent over Kenny.

"Don't get up! Jus' lay there a minute. An' fer chrissake, don't rub yer left eye! I think there's broken glass in there!"

The viciousness of what Jake had just done suddenly hit me. I stooped down below the pinsetting machine and looked up the alley at Jake, who was standing at the foul line with a nasty grin on his face.

"ARE YOU CRAZY? DO YOU KNOW WHAT YOU'VE JUS..." A dirty hand clamped firmly across my mouth before I could finish.

Mutt whispered fiercely in my ear. "Shaddup! Don'cha know who yer yellin' at? Haven't you ever seen his wife on a Sunday mornin'? D'you think he wouldn't belt you one if he felt like it?"

Mutt was right. Jake Hovi had a reputation for getting ugly mean when he had a few beers. It was common knowledge that he slapped his wife around whenever the urge came on him. Ruby Hovi frequently showed up at the Lutheran church on Sunday morning wearing dark glasses and a lot of makeup. But it couldn't cover up the agony that she had gone through the night before.

Mutt and I got Kenny home, and his mother looked at his eye and nose. Miraculously, none of the broken glass had gotten into his eye, but she had an interesting time pulling out some pieces from his eyebrow and cheek. His nose had swollen up like a balloon, but it didn't seem to be broken. She doused him liberally with iodine, stuffed some toilet paper into one of his nostrils, and let it go at that. All in all, considering how fast Jake threw that bowling ball, I figured that Kenny got off pretty lucky. The real casualty was that it took the Hukalas a couple of weeks to scrape up enough money to make a down payment for a new pair of glasses.

But the strangest part of the whole incident was the way Mutt behaved. When we brought Kenny home, Mutt told his mother that Kenny shouldn't have been in the pit when the ball was thrown and that it was all an accident. Kenny hotly objected, but Mutt just said to his mother that his younger brother didn't know enough about setting pins, or bowling, for that matter. I couldn't believe what I was hearing, but kept my mouth shut. Why would Mutt lie? He was never one to walk away from something like that. I had seen him go toe-to-toe with much bigger kids in the schoolyard for much less reason than this. But, then again, Jake Hovi outweighed him by about one hundred and sixty pounds. There was one thing that Mutt wasn't, and that was stupid.

I didn't do much pinsetting after that Saturday night. I didn't want to be around when Jake Hovi again decided that the pin boy wasn't setting them up good enough to suit him. Besides, the weather was turning cold, and my uncle Arvid was guiding me through the intricacies of laying out a weasel trap line, so I didn't have much time after school.

The business at the bowling alley continued to boom. Things really took off when Stubby set up a bowling league. In no time at all, he had enough guys for an eight-team scratch league. That worked so well that he set up a mixed-handicap league to bring in the women. Pretty soon, every weeknight was taken with league bowling. Stubby brought in an extra refrigerator and his wife served up egg-salad and ham-and-cheese sandwiches, so you didn't even have to go home to eat before your league started.

Mutt continued to set pins even after Kenny's "accident." In fact, he spent more time than ever at the bowling alley. He got to be one of Stubby's regular pin boys and talked Stubby into letting him set double alleys. Setting double alleys meant that, during league play, one pin boy would set pins on Lanes One and Two. As soon as you lifted the machine on Lane One, you had to jump over into the Lane Two pit and set them up there. You had to be very quick because it was twice the work, but you doubled your money. I'd go back to the pits every so often to visit Mutt, but he was so busy that he never had time to do much talking.

But, the talk of the town was Jake Hovi. He had taken to bowling like a duck takes to water. He had immediately joined the scratch league, and it soon became pretty clear that he was going to be the best bowler in the league. Jake could string strikes together with ease, but the most interesting thing was the way he did it. Almost every good bowler has a hook on the ball and aims for the "pocket." The "pocket" is just to the right of the center of the headpin for a right-handed bowler and vice versa for a leftie.

But, Jake just reared back and fired the ball right down the center of the alley, straight as an arrow, hitting the headpin dead on. Now, a normal bowler, doing that, would get the pins parting like the Red Sea and wind up with a split. Jake just threw the ball so hard that he blew the pins over. I hated his guts, but I had to admit that it was interesting to watch him bowl. Kind of like watching Dizzy Dean striking out batters with blistering fast balls right down the center of the plate. He was only so-so on picking up spares, but he'd get so many strikes that, as the weeks went by, his average crept up toward 200.

The only times that kids had a chance to bowl was right after school or Saturday afternoons. I'd bowl a game every now and then, but I wasn't very good at it, and I didn't have enough money to take it up seriously.

Mutt, on the other hand, bowled every chance he had. Stubby gave his regular pin boys a special deal. They could bowl for free as long as they set pins for each other. For a kid, Mutt got to be pretty good. He didn't throw the ball very fast and didn't get many strikes, but he got good at picking up spares, and as the weeks went by, Mutt got so he could hit 140 pretty regularly.

Then, one Thursday night in December, during the men's scratch league, Jake Hovi got red-hot and shot a 661 for three games and boosted his season average to 202. Even the kibitzers, who had seen him do it many times before, couldn't believe it. Jake threw ball after ball right down the center, hitting the headpin smack in the middle, and got his thunderous, magical strikes. That night, one of his cronies started to call him Headpin Hovi, and the name stuck.

To make matters even more exciting, he got a write-up in the sports page of *The Marquette Daily Mining Journal* the next day. Jake had become an overnight celebrity. After that, people would flock into the bowling alley on Thursday nights just to watch Jake bowl. Jake's money was no good at the bar. Guys would line up to buy him beers so they could get tips on how he pulled off his famous headpin strikes. Jake's answer was always the same. Throw the ball fast enough, keep it in the center of the alley, and things will take care of themselves.

Women who, up to now, had absolutely no interest in bowling, started to come in just to watch him arc the ball way over his head and smoke it down the alley. Guys who, up to now, had absolutely no interest in bowling, started to come in just to watch the women. Stubby was making money hand over fist.

The last Thursday in January was Sweepstakes Night in the men's scratch league. This was the midway point of league play and Jake's team, the Spruce Grove Tavern Muskrats, who were in first place, were going to battle it out with the second-place team, the Kloman Keglers. The Keglers had some good bowlers, but nobody gave them much of a chance that night because of Jake Hovi. Jake's average was now 206, and he was sure to be the deciding factor. The guy with the high series that night would win twenty-five dollars, and Jake was a shoo-in to take the money.

But, there was further reason for high excitement. A guy who ran Walleye Lanes in Munising was putting together an Upper Peninsula All-Star bowling team to compete in a state-wide tournament in Flint, and he was driving over to see Jake bowl that night. The word was that, if he liked what he saw, Jake was on the team.

The bowling alley started to fill up around four-thirty since seats would be at a premium. Stubby had closed down all four lanes until league play started at eight, so that he could get them cleaned and buffed down properly for the big night. Jake got there at six o'clock, and Stubby gave him an egg-salad sandwich and a Stroh's on the house. Guys were crowding around him wanting to know how he felt. Since Jake had always treated people like dirt, he had slipped into his starring role with relative ease. He sat at the bar and brushed off questions with curt answers and accepted free beers with no comment.

I was standing at the fringes, nursing a Nesbitt's Orange that was going to have to last me all evening, when I saw Mutt Hukala walk up to Jake.

"Hey, Headpin, wanna bowl a warmup game with me?"

The Nesbitt's bottle stopped halfway up to my mouth. Mutt must have hated Jake worse than I did. Why in the hell would he want to bowl with him?

Jake took a long drag off of his Camel and blew the smoke in Mutt's face. "Get lost, kid."

Stubby glared at Mutt. "Whazza matter with you, Mutt? Can'cha see I'm gettin' the alleys buffed? G'way an' don't bother people."

Mutt didn't move, but kept looking at Jake. "Aww, I'll bet Headpin'd talk ya into openin' up one of the alleys if the price was right. I hear that you like to bowl people fer money. Izzat right, Headpin?"

Jake snorted with amusement. "Tha's right, kid. But, I'm fresh out of nickels right now, so I guess that lets you out."

Mutt dug into a pocket and pulled out a twenty-dollar bill. "How about twenty bucks fer one game? You gotta gimme about thirty pins though."

I almost dropped my Nesbitt's bottle on the floor. Twenty bucks!!! I had never even held a twenty-dollar bill in my life! Had Mutt completely lost his mind?

Jake looked at the twenty in Mutt's hand and then at Mutt. A slow smile spread across his face. "Wha'ja do kid? Roll yer ol' man last Saturday night when he was drunk?"

"Nope! The money's mine. Ask Stubby. He gimme this twenty yesterday."

Stubby chimed in. "Yeah, it's his money a'right. He's been settin' pins for me since last fall, an' I been holdin' his money for him. Yesterday he asked for all of his back wages at once. I give 'im the twenty."

Mutt kept staring at Jake. "Course, maybe twenty bucks is a li'l steep for ya, Headpin."

By now, everybody had stopped whatever they were doing and were listening to the dialog between the crazy kid and Headpin Hovi. Jake's face started to turn red.

"You gotta a real smart mouth fer a snot-nosed kid! It'd serve ya right if I took that twenty away from you! I could give you sixty pins an' still wipe the floor with you!"

"Thirty's all I need. I been watching ya bowl fer a long time, now. You got the dumbest-lookin' strike ball I ever seen! I figure that you been bowlin' over yer head fer a long time, an' you're 'bout due for a fall."

I couldn't believe my ears! Was Mutt tired of living? Jake could reach out and knock his block off with one swipe of those huge hands.

Everybody in the bowling alley held their breath. Nobody talked that way to Jake Hovi! This runty kid had only seconds to live!

But Jake just stared at the twenty in Mutt's palm, drained the last swallow out of his Stroh's bottle, and got up from the bar stool.

"Somebody's gotta teach you some manners, kid, an' I'm jus' the guy t'do it." He pulled out a wallet from a hip pocket and slapped a twenty-dollar bill on the counter. "Put cher money up here an' Stubby'll hold the bets. One game fer twenty bucks! I'll give you thirty pins." He turned to Stubby. "Stubby, open up Lane One."

"But, Jake, I'm still buffing..."

"OPEN UP LANE ONE, GAWDAMMIT!"

Stubby motioned to one of the other pin boys who ran down to the pits. Jake picked his bowling bag and strode over to Lane One. He had just bought himself a new ball, perfectly fitted with extra-large finger holes. He put it on the ball return, and its shiny ebony finish had a lethal gleam. Mutt picked up one of the ladies' house balls that he had been using regularly.

Jake looked at the ladies' ball and snorted. "Sure that ain't too heavy for ya?"

The pins on Lane One were racked, and without asking for the honors of going first, Jake grabbed his ball, took aim, and fired it down the alley. The ball headed straight at the head pin, but tailed off just a fraction into the pocket. The pins exploded. Strike! With a wolfish grin, Jake sat down.

Mutt got up and went into his slow, deliberate approach. He hit the headpin light and was left with the four, seven, and eight pins for a spare. He threw the second shot too far to the right and only picked up the eight pin. After the first frame, Jake had a strike and Mutt had eight. I went up to the bar and invested in another Nesbitt's Orange to drown my sorrows.

Jake started the second frame by grooving his smoking fast ball right where he wanted it, dead on into the head pin.

But, a strange thing happened. He didn't get his usual thundering strike. He got a six-seven-ten split. He stood at the foul line and glared at it. His second shot got the six and seven pins, but he had an open frame.

Mutt got a spare in the second frame, so the game got a little interesting. Of course, it was only a matter of time before Jake would start stringing strikes together.

Jake got a spare in the third, and Mutt got nine pins on his first ball but missed the ten pin on the spare try. Jake was pulling away again.

Then, in the fourth frame, it happened again. Jake blasted the headpin straight on in his characteristic style, but got another split. He picked up nine pins and had another open frame. He yanked a Camel out of his shirt pocket, lit it, and puffed away furiously. Mutt got a spare, and the crowd that had gathered around to watch Headpin Hovi put the smart-alec kid away grew restive. Headpin wasn't off to a good start tonight. Would he get back on his game when the league started?

In the fifth frame Jake almost got a four-ten split but was saved when a rolling pin knocked over the ten pin at the last second. He picked up the spare, but one thing was clear. Headpin Hovi wasn't on his game tonight.

Mutt only picked up nine pins in the fifth, so he was about ten pins behind Jake. But, Jake had given him a thirty-pin handicap, and there were only five frames left.

The cigarette smoke grew thick as the crowd watched the game with fascination. Pike O'Neill, one of Jake's teammates on the Spruce Grove Tavern Muskrats, handed Jake a fresh, cold Stroh's.

Headpin Hovi wasn't on his game tonight...

"Drink up an' relax, Jake. Yer jus' havin' a slow start. String some strikes together, an' show this runt how it's done!"

Jake took the beer and drained half of it in one swallow. He got up on the approach and really scorched one down the center of the alley. I had never seen a bowling ball move so fast. He hit the headpin dead on.

A seven-ten split. The crowd gasped.

The final result was inevitable. Jake shot a 143 for the game. Mutt had a 139, but with the thirty-pin handicap, he beat Jake easily with a 169. A thirteen-year-old kid had just beaten one of the best bowlers in the Upper Peninsula!

Jake curled his lip as Stubby handed Mutt both twenty- dollar bills. "You got reeeeel lucky, kid. I ain't shot a game that bad since last fall!"

Mutt gave him a deadpan look. "Think it was luck, Jake? It's still early. You wanna go double or nuthin' on another game? Same rules."

Forty dollars!!! Now I knew that Mutt had lost his mind! Beating Jake in one game was a once-in-a-lifetime stroke of luck, but to try it again...!

Jake's eyes bugged out, and his face broke into an evil grin. He turned to Stubby.

"Stubby, I'm a li'l short a cash. Lend me forty dollars."

" Jake, I only got 'bout eighty dollars in the till..."

"Dammit! This is money in the bank! You think there's any chance that this punk's goin' t'beat me again?"

"OK...OK..." Stubby shook his head at Mutt. "Mutt, if yer ol' man knew that you were throwin' away forty dollars on one game of bowling, he'd kill ya!"

Mutt gave the two twenties back to Stubby, and he and Jake went over to Lane One. Somebody had given Jake another beer. The crowd of kibitzers was buzzing. Betting on the games was common...beers, small change, even a dollar or two...but, forty dollars!

Mutt turned to Jake with a lopsided grin.

"It's the Lapland Curse."

Jake took the bottle of Stroh's away from his mouth. "What?"

"That's why yer bowlin' so bad. It's the Lapland Curse."

"What the hell are'ya talkin' about, kid?"

Mutt went on. "Remember last fall when the lil' kid had crawled out on the alley to pick up some fallen pins, an' you threw the ball at him? Well, that was my kid brother. A coupla years ago, before she died, my grandmother, who came from Lapland, showed me how to put the Lapland Curse on people. To get even fer what you did to Kenny, I've put the Lapland Curse on yer bowling. You'll never bowl 200 again."

Jake had taken a mouthful of beer while Mutt was talking, and he sprayed all over the approach when he laughed.

"Har! Har! Har! You got a real knack fer crap, kid! But, it ain't gonna help ya on this game! I'm gonna take that Lapland Curse an' shove it up yer bum!" And with that, Jake grabbed his ball, took aim, and fired it down the alley. The pins exploded.

He had a seven-ten split left standing.

As it turned out, Mutt didn't need the thirty-pin handicap. In fact, he didn't need any handicap at all. He beat Jake 146 to 138. Jake had five splits in the game and some of the kibitzers said that this may have been a record for the number of splits in one game. Everybody in the house was in a state of shock except Mutt, who calmly pocketed the eighty dollars and went back to the pits to set pins for the league.

The Kloman Keglers wiped out the Spruce Grove Tavern Muskrats three games straight and took over first place in the men's scratch league. Jake shot 142, 139 and 133 for the three games and had a grand total of thirteen splits. The guy who owned Walleye Lanes in Munising watched the first two games and left. Nobody ever saw him again.

At first, people said that the kid had spooked Jake into having a really bad night and that he'd snap out of it. But, as the weeks went by, Jake just couldn't get back on track and his average plummeted. The kibitzers showered him with a blizzard of advice. Start throwing a hook...go into a five-step approach instead of four steps...throw slower...throw faster...get a new ball...get new bowling shoes.

Jake was desperate, and he started listening to everybody, which probably made matters even worse. One Thursday night, when he was convinced that he hadn't been throwing hard enough, he got one of the most unusual strikes ever seen. While bowling on Lane Four, Jake let go with a particularly violent follow-through. The ball sailed through the air, bounced once halfway down the left-hand side of Lane Four, crossed over onto Lane Three, and knocked all of the pins down. An argument immediately erupted as to whether the guy who happened to be bowling on Lane Three at the time could get credit for the strike.

While all of this was happening, the Lapland Curse was taking on a large measure of credibility. Grownups and kids alike were unusually respectful around Mutt. Even the teachers at school, to whom violence was second nature, didn't hound him when he failed to get his homework in on time. One night when Jake had downed about eight beers at the Spruce Grove, he loudly declared that he was going to tear Mutt apart for what he did to his bowling game. He was quietly advised that it probably wasn't such a good idea to mess around with anybody who was on speaking terms with demons from Lapland. Jake never followed up on his threat.

Some people decided that the Lapland Curse could be very useful. Old man Rovaniemi offered Mutt fifty cents to put a curse on Porky Sullivan's Irish Setter, who was inclined to dig up gardens all over the neighborhood. Hake Kaali wanted to know what Mutt would charge to paralyze his wife's tongue. Mutt just smiled and politely turned them down.

Then one day Jake was gone. Ruby Hovi had come home from church one Sunday and found that Jake had thrown some clothes in his old pickup truck and taken off for parts unknown. Apparently, his fall from grace had been more than he could handle. Ruby waited around for a week and then got a job in the Red Owl store. Most people agreed that this was the first time they had seen her smile in years.

One Saturday afternoon in mid March I went to the bowling alley and down into the pits. Things were a little slow, and Mutt was setting pins for Janie La Fleur and her younger brother, Tony. Both of them were just learning to bowl.

I waved my hand in greeting. "Howzit goin', Evil Eye?"

"Don't call me that. It sounds dumb."

"Dumb? You're the guy who put such a curse on Headpin Hovi that he finally left town. Evil Eye sounds about right to me."

Mutt sat on the walkway and swung his legs back and forth. He turned and gave me a crooked grin. "You mean t'say you believe all that crap about curses too?"

"What else is there to believe?"

Mutt patted the walkway next to where he was sitting. "Siddown an' I'll show ya something."

Tony La Fleur had just thrown a ball that was headed off to the right side of the alley and was likely to pick up the six, nine, and ten pins at best. At the precise time that the ball hit the six pin, Mutt swung his legs out toward the machine to avoid getting them hit by the pins, just like he had taught me to do when I was learning the trade many months ago. But there was one difference. The heel of Mutt's right shoe lightly tipped the top of the seven pin which slowly toppled over and took two others with it. If I hadn't been sitting three feet away from him, I never would have even seen it. Instead of having seven pins to shoot at with his second ball, Tony only had four. He squealed with delight at the "lucky" fall of the pins.

"What'ja do that for?"

Mutt had jumped down in the pit and was scooping up the pins. "Well, when I first started setting pins I figured out that I could make money faster if the bowlers got more strikes an' didn't have t'throw a second ball. So I started tipping pins with my foot on their first shot just to move the games along a lil' faster."

"But, can't they see you doin' it?"

"Naw. You jus' now barely saw it yourself, an' you were sittin' right here. The bowler's much further away an' the tops a the pins are in the shadow of the machine. Anyhow, when Jake clobbered Kenny that night, I had a much better reason fer doin' it."

"Whaddaya mean?"

"Well, how wuz I goin' t'get back at Jake? He's three times my size. So I decided to build him up and then let 'im fall."

"You mean...you started tipping pins fer Jake?"

"All the time. Remember that I started setting double alleys after the league started. Every time Jake threw a ball I was at the other end settin' pins fer him. An' helpin' him knock 'em down, too."

"So...all those strikes that Jake wuz gettin'...that wuz you?"

Mutt hopped back up on the walkway. "Jake Hovi wuz never a good bowler. He threw the ball fast, but he wasn't good. So, I gave 'im a li'l help. Jake couldn't average 150 on his own. He throws too many split balls."

"But, what wuz all this business 'bout the Lapland Curse?"

"I jus' said that to be funny. The Lapland Curse was when I stopped tippin' pins fer Jake on Sweepstakes Night. Boy! You wouldn't believe some of the propositions that I got! One lady, whose name I won't mention, offered me ten bucks if I could arrange it so her old man'd never get another hard-on fer the rest a his life!"

"But...Jake throws so many splits. You can't make a strike happen jus' by tippin' the seven pin."

This time Mutt's face broke into a truly proud grin.

"Ahh...but you ain't seen my best pin tipping. Watch this!"

Janie La Fleur had just thrown her ball. It was drifting off to the left and going to miss the headpin entirely. As the ball lightly grazed the two pin, Mutt swung both legs out at right angles, tipping the ten pin with his left heel and the seven pin with his right heel. All of the pins toppled in a disorganized pile on the alley.

I had to admit, Mutt was a true artist.

The nine-year-old girl jumped up and down at the foul line, clapping her hands with glee.

"A STRIKE! A STRIKE! I GOT MY FIRST STRIKE!"

The Kloman Inferno

he sign read:

DON'T EVEN THINK ABOUT PARKING HERE!

What was this? I had to check it out. Nobody ever told you where to park and not to park in this town. I had just deposited my Avis Oldsmobile among a random gaggle of pickup trucks in front of the Post Office. The town doesn't have any parking meters, loading zones or, for that matter, curbs. Even if it had such cosmopolitan amenities, there wasn't anyone appointed to write up violations. Driving and parking is a casual business in my hometown in the middle of the iron-mining region in the Upper Peninsula of Michigan where I struggled through my youth. A lone traffic light at the main intersection has been blinking yellow for years, serving as a beacon for the pulp cutters who drive up in their flatbed trucks from the surrounding woods looking for the Spruce Grove Tavern, where they come to dilute the sawdust in their gullets.

I had pulled into town the night before, making my annual sojourn from Southern California to visit my elderly mother during the September window of opportunity, after the Cessna-sized mosquitoes have retreated back into the swamps to await next year's tourists, and before the first Arctic Express comes roaring in off of Lake Superior.

The sign that had startled me was tacked to the garage door of the Township Hall, next to the Post Office. I peered through a window. My God! There was a fire engine in there! The light inside the building was dim and I had to strain to pick out the details. It's always hard to tell just how old fire engines are, but this one looked to be of pretty recent vintage. Crowned with red bubble lights, it had a siren mounted in its nose and sported thousands of chrome accessories and gauges—all mysterious and shiny. It sat there in edgy alertness, ready for duty: a lean, mean, fire-fighting machine.

My pulse quickened perceptibly, and although it was a balmy autumn morning, a deep chill seeped into my bones. A memory cascaded back into my consciousness: one morning some forty years ago, when I served in the ranks of the local fire-fighting forces...

"Hey! Get up!" My old man jabbed a finger into the three layers of blankets I had piled on top of me. I got the finger jab every school day morning, but this morning something was different. His voice had a slightly higher pitch and a greater sense of urgency. When I stuck my head out from underneath the mountain of covers, I could see my breath. Seeing your breath indoors wasn't a big deal when I was a kid—we hadn't even heard of central heating—but the timing was all wrong. We had two wood-burning stoves which the old man would stoke up to raging capacity just before we went to bed in the winter. While it was usually a nice toasty 75-80 degrees at bedtime, the fires died during the night, and in weather like we were having in January 1948, the predawn temperature could easily plummet to 25 degrees in my bedroom. Like clockwork, the old man would jump out of bed at four-thirty every morning and breathe life back into the stoves, so that by the time he prodded me for school, the inside of the house was again fit for human habitation.

"What time is it?" I asked.

"Get up! We got a chimney fire. You gotta go over and get the fire truck."

I swung my legs out of bed and struggled into the woolen pants I had dropped on the floor the night before. The big metal alarm clock on my dresser said five o'clock. A telephone and a car were indulgences that my father thought that we were doing very nicely without, so this was going to be strictly a pedestrian operation.

When I walked into the kitchen, my mother, in her chenille bathrobe and curlers, was giving the old man the benefit of her wisdom on wood stove fires.

"Why do you always have to put so much wood in it?"

"Chrissake! It's 28 below out there!" he explained.

"Did you figure you were going to warm it up a little by burning the house down?"

When it came to face-to-face verbal encounters, the old man was no match for her, but he used the urgency of the moment to fend her off and turned to me instead.

"You know where Felix Arquette lives?"

"Sure," I said, buttoning up my quarter-inch thick J. C. Penney woolen plaid shirt.

"Well, go and get him outta bed and tell him to get that fire truck over here."

The old man put the palm of his hand on the chimney above the stovepipe connection from the kitchen stove.

"Jeez! It's gettin' hotter. Hurry up!"

A chimney fire is just exactly that: a fire inside the chimney. While chimneys are certainly capable of withstanding heat, if the soot and gunk that collects in there over the years catches on fire and burns long enough, the outside of the chimney can get so hot that the roof catches fire. A chimney fire, then, is nothing to mess around with.

I put on my sheepskin coat, jammed my cap on my head, and made for the door.

"Put yer ear flaps down. It's 28 below out there!"

I stepped out into the darkness. The air hit my face like an alcohol bath. As I plodded along the footpath out to the road, the snow squeaked under my boots. We lived in the Kloman section of town, the location of the long-abandoned Kloman iron mine, dotted with aging wood-frame houses similar to ours. A full moon gave the snow a bluish haze like an old neon sign, complete with flicker.

Flicker? I whipped my head around and looked at our chimney. Flames and sparks were shooting up as if out of some gigantic, unadjusted blow torch.

Jeeeeeees.........sus!!!!!!!!!!!!!!

I broke into a frenzied gallop down the road toward the center of town. The township gravel truck had made the rounds the night before, tossing haphazard shovelfuls of sand on the street surfaces of hard-packed snow, so I zigzagged along from one sand splotch to the next to get the best traction I could.

It suddenly hit me that I was involved in an honest-to-God fire, and furthermore, the safety of house and family was entirely in my hands! That realization packed more of a wallop than the three shots of whiskey I had slugged down over at Punk Valentti's house the afternoon we conducted a raid on his old man's liquor supply during the Christmas vacation.

As I ran, the whole scenario began to unfold in my mind's eye. The story title in *The Marquette Daily Mining Journal* would read:

BOY ALERTS FIRE DEPARTMENT TO
PRE-DAWN CHIMNEY FIRE

No—no—That didn't have any class at all...

LAD ASSISTS FIRE CREW IN
EXTINGUISHING PREDAWN BLAZE

No—that wasn't quite right either. The headline of the mid-morning extra edition would read...

MAN RESCUES PARENTS FROM KLOMAN INFERNO

—While fire fighters wrestled futilely with frozen equipment in predawn sub-zero temperature, a man braved a raging blaze in his Kloman residence to bring his parents out to safety unassisted. His mother wept with relief...

Actually, the last time I had seen my mother weep was when my old man came staggering home after a three-day bender—she had taken a swing at him with his spring-steel truss and missed.

One part of this scenario was certainly true: the sub-zero temperature. While I was running, several beads of sweat popped out on my forehead and immediately froze into ice pellets. My lungs felt like they were being sandblasted, so I slowed down to a trot as I turned onto Fire Street.

Some civic-oriented committee has long since given formal names to all of the streets in town, but at that time some of the streets were referred to by whatever buildings were on them. The firehouse was on Fire Street.

The firehouse had been built in the 1890's when the town was a thriving iron-mining center. For a period of time it had served as both a firehouse and a jail, with the jail cells on the second story. But in 1948, after the town discovered it couldn't support a self-respecting jail, the building had become a repository for the fire truck and miscellaneous support equipment. It hadn't been graced with a coat of paint in decades, and its wooden exterior had weathered to a drab black-brown, matching the sparrows that perched on its eaves in search of meager winter hand-outs.

Felix Arquette was the Chief of the Township Volunteer Fire Department. The qualifications for the job didn't include a vast knowledge of dealing with chemical or electrical fires, the safety considerations of entering a burning building, or medical procedures for reviving asphyxiated fire victims. Felix held the post for the simple reason that he lived across the street from the firehouse.

Felix's house and the firehouse were at the bottom of a hill on Fire Street with the street sloping steeply upward in both directions. The gravel truck had evidently run out of sand before it got to Fire Street, and the surface was covered with a thin layer of glare ice on top of hard-packed snow. I sat on my fanny on the slippery surface and slid down the hill to land right at Felix's front porch. The house was totally dark, and I went up the steps of the porch and hammered on the glass-paned door for a minute or so.

"Whoizzit...and what the hell you want?"

I identified myself. "We gotta chimney fire!"

I had known Felix for years and was fully aware that I had just gotten him out of bed, but I wasn't prepared for the jolt of seeing him face to face the first thing in the morning, when he ripped back the curtains on the ice-rimmed window of the porch door.

Felix was of French-Canadian background with the build and disposition of a Green Bay Packers' linebacker. He had a large, square head mounted on a massive set of shoulders. His thinning, dark hair was streaked with gray, but what he was losing on the top of his head was more than compensated for by immense bushy eyebrows and the heaviest beard I had ever seen. His mother used to circulate the story that Felix had needed a shave a week after he had been born.

So, what I saw staring through the glass was the Wolfman after a three-day binge. The door opened suddenly, and I let out an involuntary squeak. I hesitated a fraction of a second too long—a giant hairy fist grabbed the front of my sheepskin and almost jerked me out of my galoshes into the living room.

"You gonna stand out there all day and let the heat out?"

He was right. It was a nice, balmy 20-25 degrees in the living room. I took my first look at the inside of Felix's house. His wife had died several years earlier, and he had redone the place with a more masculine theme.

The room was highlighted by a nice cord of wood piled against the far wall, flanked by the corpses of several browning Christmas trees in various states of dissection and a miscellaneous array of rough-hewn two-by-four's armed with rusty nails. A thick carpet of spruce needles, bark, and splinters led over to a large cast-iron heating stove with isinglass windows embedded in the door. An ancient leather easy chair sat next to a four-foot-high, wooden, Zenith floor-model radio which was sprouting a crop of empty Stroh's beer bottles. The respectable daffodil-print wallpaper next to the radio was liberally speckled with dried Stroh's foam. Clearly, Felix wasn't into hosting social engagements.

As I closed the door, Felix, in his long underwear, quickly strode over to the woodpile. One of the buttons on the trap door of his underwear was undone, and I glimpsed a patch of hairy butt. He ripped a handful of boughs from one of the hapless Christmas trees and neatly snapped a wicked-looking two-by-four in half across his knee. "Christ-all-mighty! How cold is it?"

I fended off a barrage of flying splinters with my forearm. "My old ma—my father—said it's 28 below."

Felix shoved the boughs and the pieces of two-by-four into the cold stove and scooped up a box of wooden matches from the floor. He pulled one out of the box and, as if to demonstrate that the trap door was open by design and not accident, inserted it into the open flap, swiped it across his rump, and withdrew the lit match. The boughs exploded into a full-fledged blaze, and he slammed the stove door shut.

Felix shot me an evil, bloodshot eye. "A chimney fire, huh? Don't your old man ever clean the damn thing out?"

"Uh—I dunno. He just told me to come over here and get you to bring the truck."

"Gawd!!! I'll never get 'er started in this weather. Look, I'm gonna call up a coupla guys, an' you go out there and turn it over."

My heart froze. Starting up the fire truck! The situation came into clear focus. We're roaring across the Kloman bridge, siren screaming, me at the wheel, Felix and the others standing on the rear platform of the truck, while the flames from the house cast an eerie flicker onto our polished helmets firmly secured with chin straps.

I was still a year and a half short of legal driving age, but I'd already logged in a few covert hours behind the wheel of my uncle's '46 Chevrolet, not to mention my being a feverish observer of the start-up procedures of any car that I rode in these days. As a result, I had compiled a vast store of knowledge on the ignition, starter, and gear locations of every make and model. Given the opportunity, I could start up any car in town.

"Where's the key?" I squeaked.

"What?"

I shifted my voice into a lower register. "Where's the key to the truck?"

Felix furrowed his eyebrows as he tried to make some sense out of the question. "No, gawdammit! What I wantcha to do is go out there and turn the motor over a coupla times with the crank. That motor oil'll be stiffer than your cock if it's 28 below! Ain't nobody starts up that truck besides me!"

I sagged, but this was still heady business. "Where's the crank?"

Felix's lip started to curl. "IT'S STUCK IN THE FRONT END A THE TRUCK! WHERE THE HELL DIDJA THINK IT WAS?"

I could see that I was losing his confidence, so I scurried for the door. Felix had already grabbed the telephone and was jabbing the cradle to wake up the Marquette County operator.

The only fringe benefit of being a volunteer fireman was a township-subsidized telephone, but that was so highly prized there was never any shortage of applicants. A telephone was a symbol of affluence, and even for some, a source of entertainment. Making a long-distance call was often a social occasion where relatives, friends, and neighbors would come over to see if you got through to talk to Aunt Rose in Grand Rapids. Less fortunates would drop by on any pretext just to look at it, hoping it would ring while they were there.

As I was going out the door, I heard Felix already badgering the operator.

"HELLO?—HELLO? GAWDAMMIT—ARE YOU AWAKE? THIS IS THE FIRE CHIEF IN..."

The headline of the midmorning extra would read...

I ran down the front steps and across the street to the firehouse. A dim forty-watt street lamp lit up the front of the building. It must have been a slack time for fires because there was at least a foot of snow in the driveway. The only concession to the twentieth century was an overhead hinged garage door, procured at no small expense from Montgomery Ward in Marquette.

I waded into the snow, reached down, and tugged at the garage door handle. It didn't budge. Ice and frost had welded it to the door frame. I attacked it with a vengeance, kicking, pounding, using every word and phrase in my rich vocabulary of expletives. In a moment of impropriety I shucked my wool-lined leather choppers and grabbed the metal door handle with my bare hand. Like the proverbial tongue on the pump handle, it stuck fast. I recited three sonovabitches and two gawdammits, gritted my teeth, and tore it loose, leaving a good six square inches of skin behind and permanently altering the fingerprints on my right hand.

I had to stop and rest. Although the weather was frigidly cold, I was well insulated, and the exertion had started to percolate my usual gamy wintertime body oil which, when mixed with the natural barnyard essence of the sheepskin coat, resulted in a bouquet oozing up from my collar reminiscent of a Chicago stockyard.

The snow squeaked behind me, and I turned to see Felix coming across the street. His fire-fighting gear consisted of an old mackinaw with a deer license still safety-pinned to the back, a billed, wool hunting cap with lowered ear flaps, and rubber swampers on his feet. He had retrieved a half-smoked cigar from somewhere and puffed on it furiously as he approached. His brows were knitted together in a furry horizontal line and bared yellow teeth clenched the mangled cigar. Felix definitely had his game face on.

"HOW THE HELL YOU EVER 'SPECT TO BE A FIREMAN IF YA CAN'T OPEN THE GAWDAMM FIRE HOUSE DOOR?" He reared back with a massive, booted leg and dealt the garage door a thunderous kick. The building shuddered violently with sheets of snow cascading from the roof. Drowsy sparrows chittered in confusion, not knowing what to do before sunrise. He reached down for the handle and with wood squawking against wood, opened the garage door.

And there in the gloom, in an advanced state of hibernation, sat the township fire truck. It was a 1930 Model A Ford dressed in oxidized red. It had an open cockpit with retractable wooden ladders mounted on each side of a large, cylindrical water tank. Either the tank was empty, or else it held a very large ice cube. Hoses were stored in a hand-made wooden box bolted to a rear platform, which also served as a place to stand. The truck was perched on lofty 4.75"x19" tires mounted on spoked wheels with four-inch hubcaps. It looked as if it was ready for anything but movement.

Felix pointed to the crank jutting out of the front end below the radiator. "Well, get in there and turn her over."

Since vintage cars were nothing new around town, I had seen this done plenty of times. So, I straddled the front bumper, took the end of the crank with both leather choppers, and threw all of my sinewy 135 pounds into the task. The crank moved about a quarter of a turn.

Felix now kissed me off as being totally nonfunctional and brushed me aside. He had the reputation of a muscle man, so I was gratified to see him grunt with exertion as he turned over the truck engine a couple of times.

Just about then, Eino Maki, one of the volunteers, strolled up. I briefed him on the fire situation. He looked at me and said: "Yer Arvid's boy, aintcha?" Since it was common practice to identify underage rabble by their parents, I accepted the affront to my identity. Until you were eighteen and holding a steady job, or got someone's daughter pregnant, few people knew your Christian name. Eino looked at Felix laboring with the crank, shook his head slowly, and fished out a sack of Bull Durham and a package of Zig-Zag papers. He quickly rolled and lit a cigarette before his fingers stiffened up from the cold.

Felix climbed into the front seat of the truck, put the gear shift into neutral, opened the gas line, pulled out the choke, adjusted the spark lever, set the manual throttle, and turned on the ignition. A Model A Ford could never be considered user friendly; it almost required a co-pilot to operate it. Muttering a couple of Hail Marys, he punched the electric starter on the floorboard with his boot. The truck emitted a ragged death moan, then a gasp, then lapsed into silence.

Eino took a drag off his cigarette and shook his head again. "That battery's deader'n hell, Felix. Did you leave it in the truck overnight?"

"Yeah, I left it in the truck! If you think that every time we get a fire call, I'm gonna come runnin' outta the house carrying that gawdamm battery in my arms, you gotta another think comin'!"

But, Eino was warming up to the task of slipping the needle to Felix. "I thought that one a tha main jobs of bein' fire chief wuz you had to take the truck battery in every night and sleep with it to keep it nice'n warm."

Felix, however, had a natural flair for assuming the position of authority. He jumped out of the truck, grabbed a snow shovel leaning up against the wall, and tossed it to Eino.

"IF YOU WANNA PUT YER ASS IN GEAR INSTEDDA YER BIG YAP, YOU CAN SHOVEL OFF THE DRIVEWAY, ON THE OFF CHANCE THAT WE GET THIS PILE A JUNK STARTED!"

A silence ensued for the next ten minutes or so while Felix tried to reverse the state of rigor mortis of the fire truck by cranking and Eino shoveled the driveway. While I stood around, I took stock of my body. The frozen sweat on my forehead was starting to hurt like hell, my right palm was turning the color of raw sirloin steak, and my near-frozen toes were saying goodbye to the rest of my feet. We hadn't even left the firehouse, and I could already have been classified as walking wounded.

Cliff Alatalo, the last member of our elite team, walked up at that moment with a large thermos bottle under his arm.

"WHERE THA HELL YOU BEEN? YUR SUPPOSED TO BE A GAWDAMM FIREMAN!" Felix roared.

Cliff gave him a knowing grin. "I knew you'd never get 'er started, so I made a pot a coffee after you called." He unscrewed the cap, poured a cup, and handed it to Eino. Eino poured it down his gullet without so much as a swallow. I gratefully accepted the first refill. I had just reached the age where I was being allowed to embark on a lifetime addiction to caffeine.

I told Cliff about the fire and he looked me over briefly. "Yer Arvid's boy, aintcha?"

Another ten minutes went by while Felix continued to attack the engine with the crank, making frequent adjustments to the choke setting. He had fished out a fresh cigar, which seemed to renew his resolve.

Cliff turned to Eino, who was now leaning on his snow shovel, and said, "How d'ya think the fire's goin', Eino?"

"I dunno. Maybe we'll read about 'er in *The Mining Journal* this afternoon."

"Yah. I figure when the sun comes up and warms up the front end a the truck, we'll getter started in no time."

That was enough for Felix. He jumped up and jabbed the crank under Cliff's nose. "Comedians, are ya? Let's see if you can do any better!"

Cliff took the crank, stared intently in at the crank hole on the truck, inserted the crank, and with one flick of the wrist brought the engine to life with a stuttering roar.

All four of us were freeze-framed for a good five seconds. Felix, who had been relighting his cigar, burned his thumb and forefinger. Eino, rolling a cigarette, dribbled half a bag of Bull Durham on the driveway. I was taking a drink of coffee and parboiled my upper lip. But Cliff just stood there, straddling the bumper, giving us a cool stare.

Then, as if on cue, we were all galvanized into action. Felix jumped into the front seat and started to adjust the engine settings. Eino grabbed the shovel and furiously attacked the remaining few feet of driveway snow to the street. Cliff scrambled away from the front end of the roaring truck in case Felix decided to put it into gear, and I jumped up and down, clapping my choppers together like some idiot. My half-frozen feet appreciated it, though.

A sudden wind had sprung up, and if we had known in those days what wind chill factors were, we would have pronounced it an invigorating 95 below zero, but my frenzied adrenal glands were making a Cinderella-like transformation of the whole scene.

Fire Street was now the aircraft carrier *USS Hornet*, making a lumbering turn into the wind for takeoffs. Like the enchanted pumpkin, the Model A fire truck was remolding itself into a powerful North American Mitchell B-25 bomber with huge twin engines revving up to full throttle. Felix's Mr. Hyde-like visage was softening into a good likeness of Spencer Tracy as Jimmy Doolittle in *Thirty Seconds Over Tokyo*, as he awaited takeoff clearance from the deck crew. The woolen earlaps on his cap were rounding into earphones.

WE WERE GOING ON A MISSION!

But, it wasn't going to be an easy one. Eino came in from the street and said, "Felix, you got chains for this truck?"

"You kiddin'? Those tight sunsabitches on the Township Board barely gimme gas money!"

"Well, I dunno then. That hill's pretty slick. They didn't throw sand on 'er last night."

Felix puffed on his cigar for a long moment. "Tha hell with it! Let's go!"

Jimmy Doolittle couldn't have put it any better.

"Can I ride on the back?" I asked Felix.

"An' have you fall off and then your old man sues me? Not a chance!" He slapped the leather seat next to him. "Up here!" I climbed in, and Eino got in after me. Another indignity—riding in the middle of the seat between two adults. Cliff got on the rear platform, and with a clash of gears Felix pulled the truck out onto the street.

I looked out through the windshield. The deck of the *Hornet* was canted up at an extreme angle. This is going to be a rough takeoff in this sea, I thought grimly. The snow on the deck is going to make it even more dangerous. Doolittle puffed on his cigar, revved up the engines to a high-pitched scream, took his foot off the brakes, and the B-25 rushed forward.

The bomber climbed up the deck but gradually started to lose power, and about fifty yards from the top, it came to a complete stop. The wheels spun madly, throwing up two rooster tails of snow.

"Gawdammit all to hell!" snapped Felix as the fire truck dug its rear wheels into the hard-packed snow. But, he was not to be daunted by the laws of physics. He quickly slammed it into reverse and started backing down the hill, fishtailing violently due to the limited visibility caused by the water tank on the back. The water tank, however, did nothing to impede the flow of air rushing up from behind. In fact, it acted like an ideal airfoil, directing the air right into the truck seat like the trailing edge of a wing. The wind chill factor now resided at a few degrees short of liquefaction.

My mouth had been hanging open since we started back down the hill, and my tongue, which had been comfortably nesting in my oral cavity at normal body temperature for fourteen and a half years, expired on the spot. My lungs analyzed the hostile alien substance screaming down my gullet and flatly refused to exchange it for carbon dioxide.

Eino, who had also made the mistake of looking back when Felix put it in reverse, now resembled one of the main characters in *Revenge of the Zombies*—which I had seen at the Delft Theater in Marquette a few weeks earlier. Felix was protecting his head with a thick cloud of pungent cigar smoke. I would have gladly taken up cigar smoking on the spot or, for that matter, lit my cap on fire if I had a match.

The fire truck sped by the firehouse in reverse and backed up the opposite hill. Felix had it in mind to employ a slingshot technique, using the gravity of the opposite hill to get a running start and propel the truck up the one that we had failed to negotiate. Halfway up the opposite hill we again spun the wheels. Felix immediately pounded the transmission into first gear, and we took another run at hill number one.

We were again on the balmy side of the maneuver with the windshield protecting us, and as we whistled past the firehouse with the truck floored in second gear, I sat there trying to slap some feeling back into my nose and cheeks.

The truck roared up the hill and made it further this time, but spun its wheels again before we got to the top. Felix threw it in reverse and had it floored in a matter of seconds. This time I put my head between my knees, having no inclination to observe the action, as the mind-numbing icy air rushed in on us from around the water tank—the amusement ride from hell.

As we rocketed past the firehouse, we undoubtedly set the world's speed record for a Model A Ford travelling in reverse. For the first time I thought of Cliff Alatalo, whom we couldn't see, but since we hadn't run over him, must have still been on the back of the truck. I idly wondered how long it might take, left to the forces of nature, for him to thaw out and fall off. It might be as late as Memorial Day.

This time we easily made it to the top of the opposite hill in reverse gear, at which time Felix brought it to a sliding stop, and putting it back into first gear, gunned the engine violently. For the first time Eino unclenched his chattering teeth. "No, Felix, you don't have to do the hill again. Back up to the corner to my house and go over to Kloman Street and get to their house that way." I nodded my head—yes—and gave a vigorous "Aauugghh huhhh."

But, backing away from this wasn't Felix's style. It had become personal with him. With the gas pedal down to the wooden floorboard, he popped the clutch, and throwing up huge geysers of snow from the rear wheels, started back down toward the firehouse.

By now, lights had started to come on in the houses along Fire Street. People were pulling back their shades to observe the struggle between man, his machine, and "The Hill." For months afterward, debates on the event would be held. Some would contend that Felix had no business making that final pass at the hill, that he should have taken the prudent way out as Eino had suggested. Others said that Felix could have easily negotiated the hill on the second attempt by a wiser sequence of gear shifting. One entrepreneur at the Spruce Grove Tavern suggested that the town make it an annual event and invite fire trucks from all over Marquette County to compete. Felix himself finally put the issue to rest by stating that he would personally kick the hell out of anyone else who ever tried it.

And so we screamed by the firehouse and assaulted the hill for the third time. My Jimmy Doolittle fantasy evaporated when reality became more life threatening than the fantasy itself; *Thirty Seconds Over Tokyo* was a walk in the park compared to this.

Felix already had it into third gear when we passed the firehouse. When the truck started to slow down on the hill, he speed-shifted into second. The truck slewed violently from one side of Fire Street to the other, the engine snarling and the rear wheels churning up snow, but we made it to the top. Felix coasted to a stop, took the soggy, mangled cigar from his mouth, leaned out of the driver's side, looked back down at the hill, and spat in the snow. Nobody or nothing screwed around with Felix Arquette.

Just then we heard a faint "Stop...stop," from the rear of the truck. Cliff walked up to us with the stiff-legged gait of Frankenstein's monster. His complexion was a startling shade of grayish-white, and his eyebrows sparkled with frost. Twin streams of mucus had flowed from his nose and had frozen into fangs below his upper lip. Gone was the self-assured, cocky individual that we had known a scant twenty minutes earlier. Cliff Alatalo was a broken man.

"Felix, Felix, don't back down the hill again! I've had it! I think I'm freezin' to death!"

Felix gave him a puzzled look. "Why should I back down the hill again? Get back on the truck! We got a fire to go to!"

"No! No! Hell, no! I can't ride back there no more!"

Felix turned and looked at me thoughtfully. I shrank down in the seat. My priorities on where to ride on the fire truck had shifted radically in a short time. He looked at Eino, who didn't look much better than Cliff.

"Then you better walk over there. It ain't far and the exercise'll warm you up." With that he put the truck into gear and took off for Kloman.

My adrenal glands were just starting to thaw when we turned the corner to the Kloman bridge. I had been gone almost an hour, and I looked across the river toward our house, expecting the worst—Klomanites pulling my parents from the blazing inferno—utter devastation.

The chimney fire was out.

The chimney had smoke curling from it, but it was just the usual by-product of a stove fire. Everything was normal! I couldn't believe it. How had things gone so utterly wrong? A raging fire was the only fitting climax to the events that had taken place. Jimmy Doolittle had taken a wrong turn from the Hornet and wound up over Honolulu! I was staring blankly out through the windshield when Eino said, "Well, kid, it looks like we got lucky."

Felix pulled the fire truck up to the path leading to the house, leaving the engine running. It would have been unthinkable to turn it off. We trudged through the back door into the kitchen.

"Where have you been?" my mother asked. This was her standard question, which I was to hear many more times before I left for college. By then the question was upgraded to "Why haven't you written?"

Felix got me off the hook. "We had a little trouble gettin' the truck started, but it looks like you got the chimney fire out anyhow."

My mother nodded her head toward the old man. "That was easy once I got him to stop putting so much wood in the stove."

My old man pulled out two wooden kitchen chairs from the table. "You fellas sit down and have some coffee." With the consummate skill of a Finnish housewife with many years of reacting to uninvited company, my mother was already dealing out cups and saucers on the table. The usual large plate of pound cake, bear claws and rusk toast appeared from its hiding place in the pantry along with a pound of butter.

"This is real butter and not that colored oleo that they're pushing these days," my mother said righteously. She then grabbed the 25-gallon enameled coffee pot from its eternal resting place on the left front stove lid, along with the strainer, and proceeded to fill up the cups. Then, as her final coup, to signify that this was not your ordinary mundane coffee spread put out for relatives and neighbors, she produced a rhubarb pie she had made the night before.

Eino had poured coffee into his saucer to cool it down to drinking temperature and was attempting to raise it to his mouth, but his hands were shaking so bad that he was slopping it on the oilcloth that covered the table.

"DRINK IT OUTTA THE CUP FER CRISSAKE! YER NOT OUT AT THE CAMP NOW!" Felix barked. "Excuse me, missus," he added, nodding to my mother.

Just then there was a knock at the kitchen door, and the old man opened it. "Who're you?"

Felix was dunking a Rusk into his coffee and didn't even look up. "That's Alatalo. He walked over."

"Jeees, I didn't recognize you," the old man exclaimed. "You look pretty cold. Come in an' have some coffee."

"Got any whiskey?" Cliff whispered. All I could see was his white nose and cheeks from under the bill of his frosty cap.

"FERGET THE WHISKEY, GAWDAMMIT! THIS IS A CHRISTIAN HOUSE-HOLD!" Felix snarled. "Excuse me, missus, but he'll be OK. Just give'm a cup a coffee."

Cliff sat down at the table and looked dumbly at the steaming coffee cup in front of him, probably wondering how he was going to get it to his mouth. However, his nose was starting to run again, which was a good sign.

Eino was just now returning from the brink of terminal hypothermia. "Felix, since we didn't have any water in the tank, just exactly where is the nearest hydrant to this house?"

Felix paused with a dripping rusk toast in his hand. "I dunno. Arvid, d'you know where it is?"

The old man thought for a few seconds. "I think there's one up at the top a the hill in those tansy weeds by Mattila's house."

"We wouldn't have enough hose on the truck to reach from there to here," said Eino.

"What difference does it make? D'you think yer goin' to get runnin' water outta that hydrant in this weather?", Felix asked.

"Then what're we doin here?" Eino said.

"We're drinkin' coffee," Felix said with finality.

I walked away from the garage door of the Township Hall, still shivering as I zipped up my L. L. Bean windbreaker.

"May I help you?"

I turned and saw a young man in his mid-twenties with a polite grin on his face. He was clean cut with tanned face and arms, and dressed in a dark blue uniform with VOLUNTEER FIRE DEPARTMENT stenciled above the left pocket of his shirt. I didn't recognize him, but he was probably the son of someone that I'd gone to school with.

"I was just admiring your fire truck," I said.

"Isn't she a beauty?" He pushed a button on a remote control unit attached to his wide leather belt and the garage door quietly slid open. The truck dazzled us in the morning sunlight.

"We just got it a few months ago. I've been checking her out, and do you know that there isn't any place in the township that I can't get this truck into?"

Yeah, I thought, but how do you think you'd do from a standing start at the bottom of Fire Street, or whatever the hell they call it nowadays, in the dead of winter, with no sand on the hard pack? How fast have you had it in reverse? Could you kick that garage door open if that fancy electronic gizmo on your belt didn't work? Hah! You may be good, kid, but I was here when they had the best.

The Navigator

I'm convinced God really has a sense of humor.

I know—I know—some people might take offense to that, but what other explanation is there for some of the bizarre things that take place on this earth? As for myself, I can recall occasions where Divine, but droll, intervention was really the only logical answer. For instance, there was the time in October 1948...

Gawd, I hope I get it right this time, I thought, as I plunked a sweaty hand on the gear shift knob. My left foot slammed in the clutch, and I pushed the gear shift into neutral. Then, I let out the clutch and gunned the motor in rapid succession. The next step was to put in the clutch again and shift it into second gear.

GGGGGGGGGRRRRRRRRRR!!!!!!!!!!!!

The transmission snarled in defiance, and my uncle Arvid, sitting in the passenger seat, gnawed on his lower lip.

"You gotta push the clutch in further."

This was not news to me, but my brain was overloaded with the combined excitement of going out on my first partridge hunt and getting a driving lesson at the same time.

I got the vehicle into second, carefully let out the clutch, and gingerly pressed down on the gas pedal. The command car bucked violently a couple of times and died. I smacked the steering wheel in frustration.

"Aaaawwwwww! I'll try 'er again!" I ground on the starter.

"Well...the road's goin' to get pretty narrow from here on in. Why don'cha let me take over now." Arvid got out and walked around to the driver's side. My hope of driving all the way out to his camp went up in a puff of smoke.

The two of us were on our way to his new camp, about fifteen miles from town, to spend the weekend partridge hunting. We were driving a U.S. Army 1943 Dodge command car that Arvid had bought at a war-surplus auction at Sault Ste. Marie the preceding winter. The command car was a burly, three-quarter-ton, four-wheel-drive machine that looked like a muscle-bound Jeep, except twice the size. For all I knew, it had been designed to storm Omaha Beach on D-Day. To erase any doubts of its ability to traverse all terrain, it had a monstrous electric winch on the front end, which could be used to pull you out of the depths of hell. It was a no-nonsense vehicle, but was a real bitch to drive, especially when you had to double clutch it to shift gears and you didn't yet qualify for a driver's license. Arvid had given me a couple of lessons on his '46 Chevy, but today, for some reason, he thought I was ready for something bigger. It was the equivalent of taking a few flying lessons in a Piper Cub and then having the flight instructor put you in the cockpit of a B-29 Superfortress.

Arvid got behind the wheel and started her back up, and we continued on our way. The road quickly narrowed as we got further into the bush. We rounded a bend and suddenly came upon a fallen jack pine blocking the road. Without saying a word, he reached down between the seats and yanked the lever engaging the four-wheel drive. The command car's power train now took on an authoritative growl, and the vehicle clambered over the jack pine like a foraging bear.

I beamed at him with teen-age admiration. "Wow! This thing's really neat! I bet there's nuthin' in the world that kin stop it!"

Just about then, God must have started to smile.

My uncle Arvid was normally a level-headed, taciturn type who rarely indulged in frivolous activities, but my open adulation of the command car must have driven him to the brink of excessive behavior. He turned to me and with a twitch of his right eye which, for him, served as a wink, said, "Wanna see a shortcut to the camp?"

"Sure!"

Abruptly, he turned the wheel to the left and headed into a wall of young poplar trees. Their trunks were about two inches thick, but this presented no match for the command car. It snapped the trees off at bumper level with nasty-sounding cracks that sounded like pistol shots. Arvid must have had a map of Marquette County etched on his brain because we proceeded into the dense bush without the benefit of a map or compass.

I was having the time of my life, living fantasies of entering uncharted territory, where no white man had ever gone. The command car climbed up a small rise, snapping trees as it crested the top with the front wheels, when...

CCCCLLLL...LLLLUUUUNNNNKKKK!!!!!!!

For reasons unknown, the command car had come to a sudden, jarring stop.

Miraculously, I had gotten my left hand up in front of my face just in time to keep my nose from smashing into the windshield.

We climbed out and inspected the wheels. They were all sitting on solid ground, with no rocks obstructing them. Nothing was in front of the bumper and, stooping down, we didn't see anything that had gotten stuck on the transmission or rear-end housing.

Then we saw it.

Somehow, when the command car had come up to the top of the small rise with its front end pointing up, the front bumper had just cleared a tree stump on the other side of the crest. When the front end came back down, the stump had gotten wedged between the bumper and the electric winch located behind it. The stump was a good seven or eight inches in diameter, so we weren't going to snap it off or pull it out by the roots with the power of the engine or the winch. The ground was too soft to support the jack to lift up the front end. We were, in a word, stuck. The only way we were going to get loose was to saw off the stump, and we didn't have a saw.

What were the chances of all this happening? About six million to one.

Like I said, God really has a sense of humor.

Arvid stood there staring at the stricken vehicle like a preacher who just caught his wife in bed with a traveling salesman. He must have thought, "How could you do this to me?"

But, in true Lutheran style, he didn't vent his emotions on a fait accompli. He calmly pulled out a sack of Bull Durham, a packet of Zig-Zag papers, and rolled himself a cigarette. He flicked his thumbnail across the head of a kitchen match and lit it.

"We'll hafta get a bucksaw an' cut off the stump."

"You have one at the camp?"

"Yeah, but that's about five miles—Smoked-Ham Sullivan's place is about half a mile from here—I think we'll go there an' borrow one."

Smoked-Ham Sullivan! This man was a legend in his own time! No one in town could remember the last time they had seen him. Some people claimed he had been shot and killed years ago by federal agents raiding his still. Others believed he never existed at all. I certainly had never seen him. The prevailing story was that he lived with a few cronies in an abandoned logging camp way out in the bush and that, once a year or so, one of his pals would steal into town and buy a year's supply of flour, salt, canned goods, and a large quantity of smoked ham. During Prohibition, he had made a comfortable living making and selling bootleg wine and whiskey. But the word was that the repeal of Prohibition hadn't really slowed him down from his chosen career and that a select clientele of local pulp cutters regularly paid him visits during the middle of the week when they couldn't get into town to the bars. Anybody who knew where Smoked-Ham Sullivan lived kept their mouth shut. My uncle Arvid, who, by the way, was a strict teetotaler, had always claimed that he knew Smoked-

Ham pretty well from when he was running trap lines before the war. Arvid wasn't given to telling tall tales, so it looked like we were going to pay Smoked-Ham Sullivan a visit.

Arvid had gone around to the back of the command car and was strapping a revolver on his waist. He reached into the back of the car and pulled out his twelve-gauge pump-action shotgun.

"Take your shotgun. We might see some birds."

I reached into the back seat and took out my single-shot twenty-gauge. Somehow, I got the impression that partridge hunting wasn't the only reason why it was a good idea to take guns along.

Instead of backtracking down the pathway that the command car had cleared and picking up the road from town, Arvid struck off at an oblique angle into the woods. I looked around. The trees looked identical in every direction. I looked up at the sky. It was its usual October slate gray with the sun nowhere to be seen. How does he do that? I was completely lost.

We trekked through the woods for about ten minutes and came out on a two-rut road almost closed in by ferns and tree branches. Arvid stopped.

"This is the road to Smoked-Ham's camp. I ain't been out here for many years, but the las' time I was here he hadda pack of dogs, so stay behind me."

He started up the road, but then, as an afterthought, he turned to me.

"An' whatever you do, if he offers you coffee, turn it down!"

We walked up the road about a quarter mile when we came upon a clearing. There were about half a dozen log structures; all but two of them were in utter disrepair. The roofs had long since fallen in, and the doors and windows were only gaping holes. The two better-looking ones weren't anything to write home about either. There were numerous chinks between the logs, the tar paper roofs had patches, and several of the windowpanes were closed up with cardboard. But, smoke drifted up from the stovepipe chimney on the larger of the two, so somebody was home.

GGRROORR...YYOOWWLL...YAPYAPYAPYAP...GGGRRR!!!

A stream of what seemed like a thousand dogs boiled out of one of the door-less log buildings and headed straight for us at top speed—a sea of ears, tails, tongues, and fangs. The tails weren't wagging.

I wanted to ask Arvid what the best strategy was, but all that came out was, "Awwwwkkk!!!" My knuckles turned white around the twenty-gauge shotgun.

The pack was led by a large, particularly mangy-looking, black mutt whose qualification for leadership was a mouthful of three-inch fangs.

BLLLAAAMMMM!!!! BLLLAAAMMMM!!!!

Arvid had cranked off two shots from his twelve-gauge, and twin geysers of dirt erupted in front of the lead dog. This was a language that the dog understood—he tried to stop, but was going much too fast, and only succeeded in tumbling ass over teakettle to land at Arvid's feet.

He scrambled to his feet with a wicked snarl, but Arvid quickly pumped another shell into the chamber and pointed the shotgun at the dog's head. The hound looked into the smoking barrel and backed away with his teeth still bared.

"My gawd! How are ya, Arvid? I ain't seen you since Moses wuz a pup!"

I tore my eyes away from the dogs to see a tall, gangly man approaching from the big log house. As he neared, I could see that this was, without a doubt, the ugliest guy I had ever seen in my life. One of his eyeballs was completely missing from the socket. All of his top teeth were gone, except for one unusually long, brown one. His nose was large and red with purplish veins laced throughout, indicating many years of boozing. His stringy gray hair looked like it had been cut with a hunting knife. He wore raggedy bib overalls over brownish, long underwear. But, the most striking thing was the fact that he was covered with blood from his elbows to his fingertips and all down the front of the overalls. This had to be Smoked-Ham Sullivan because I sure as hell would have remembered him if I had ever seen him before.

He dragged a filthy red bandanna out of his hip pocket and did a perfunctory cleaning of his bloody hands as he came up to us, a big grin displaying his solitary upper fang. He stuck out his right hand to Arvid.

"How'zit goin'? This yer kid?"

Arvid shook his blood-smeared hand. "How're ya, Smoked-Ham? No, this's my nephew."

Smoked-Ham grabbed my hand and gave me a greasy handshake. "How're ya, young fella? Goin' bird huntin', I see." Still grinning, he turned back to Arvid. "Ya could'a yelled at them dogs stead'a wastin' shells, Arvid."

"I didn't know how hungry they might be."

"Aww...they're gittin' plenty t'eat this mornin'. I'm guttin' a doe an' they're havin' a feast with the innards."

He was right. The dogs had now lost all interest in us and were scrapping ferociously over bloody entrails underneath a doe carcass, which was strung up by its front legs to a limb of a tree near the large log house. Apparently, Smoked-Ham didn't lose any sleep over the rules and regulations of deer season, which didn't start until next month.

"Cum on in! I wuz jus' goin' t'have coffee an' some fig bars." Smoked-Ham turned to the left and yelled into the woods. "HEY MUSHRAT! CUM ON IN! THEY'RE ALL RIGHT!"

About fifty yards away, a man stepped out of the woods with a 30-30 carbine cradled in his arms. He had been watching us all along.

We went into the large log building. The interior light was very dim, but it was hard to miss the gigantic, cast-iron wood stove in the center of the main room. It must have had sixteen lids on the cooking surface and was obviously a survivor of the days when this was a thriving logging camp. The room had a packed-dirt floor, and the interior walls looked just like the exterior walls—logs sealed up with packed dirt and tree moss. The furniture consisted of a rough-hewn, long table, flanked by various, mismatched kitchen chairs. A couple of old car seats were up against two walls. Ribbons of well-populated flypaper hung from the rafters.

Smoked-Ham grabbed a huge, steaming, fire-blackened coffee pot from one of the front stove lids and banged it down on the center of the table.

"Have sum coffee an' set down an' chew the fat awhile! I ain't had visitors fer a year or so!"

Arvid immediately put up his hand. "No...no coffee. We gotta get going. I just wanted to know if we could borrow a bucksaw."

"Sure! Got plenty of saws." He turned to me. "How 'bout you? Wanna a cuppa coffee?"

Before I could answer, Arvid said, "He's a bit too young to be drinking coffee."

A voice from behind me replied, "Everybody's too young to be drinkin' Smoked-Ham's coffee." The man with the carbine had come in the door. He had a huge belly with incredibly bloodshot eyes set in a round, whiskery face. His breath smelled like a hot car radiator filled with Prestone.

Smoked-Ham grinned. "This here's Mushrat Rommi." He turned to me and winked his one remaining eye. "Know why we call him Mushrat? 'Cause years ago, when we wuz runnin' a muskrat trap line, Mushrat developed a taste fer muskrat meat."

"Mushrat's purty good eatin'," said Mushrat solemnly.

Smoked-Ham continued, "Now, with fur prices bein' what they are, the only thing that it pays to trap is beaver an' mink."

"Beaver's purty good eatin' too", Mushrat added.

"Har! har! har! Mushrat'll eat anythin' that craps in tha woods! Once I seen him pan-fryin' a weasel!"

"Weasel ain't such good eatin'. Kind'a gamy."

Smoked-Ham took a coffee cup from the corner of the table and, with a deft flick of his wrist, shook the dregs onto the dirt floor. He looked around the room briefly. "Mushrat, where's that coffee strainer?"

"Ain't seen it. Why don'cha use what'cha always use? You puttin' on the dog fer company?"

Smoked-Ham grabbed a fly swatter, which happened to be lying on the top of the stove and, holding it over his coffee cup, poured a thick, black, ugly stream from the pot into the cup. My stomach lurched. The fly swatter caught the coffee grounds which tumbled out of the pot in large lumps.

"Mushrat, when's the las' time we emptied the old grounds outta this pot?"

"Dunno. Las' summer sometime."

Smoked-Ham got up and went over to an orange crate, nailed on the log wall, that served as a cupboard. He took out a can of Carnation milk, put it on the table, took a blood-smeared, eight-inch hunting knife out of his belt, and quickly punched a couple of holes in the top of the can. He poured a liberal amount in the coffee. He took a satisfying slurp of coffee and gummed a stale fig bar.

"I'd offer you sum a Mushrat's homemade bread, but it went moldy a cuppla weeks ago. It's gettin' so green it'd cure syphilis."

"That ain't the only reason we don't get syphilis out here," Mushrat said.

Smoked-Ham leaned back in his chair and let out a satisfied belch.

"So, Arvid. Whaddaya hear that's new?"

Arvid scratched his chin. "Well...we won the war."

"That's what I hear! Were you in it?"

"Yeah, they had me drivin' truck in France fer awhile."

"See any action?"

"Well...the Germans almos' got me with a V-2 one day."

"Whazzat?"

"It's a big rocket...'bout three stories high."

"Sunavabitch! An' they shot it at you? You must'a been one helluva truck driver!" Smoked-Ham turned to Mushrat. "I always said that Arvid could handle a truck real good!" He turned back to Arvid. "So, I hear you built yerself a new camp out past Fence Lake."

"Yeah, I figure to do some logging out there next year."

Smoked-Ham gave me a serious stare with his eye. "You ever been huntin' out there, young fella?"

I shook my head. "Nope."

"Well...that's purty wild country. You be careful you don't get turned around in the woods. If you pick the wrong direction, you could keep walkin' till you get to Crystal Falls, 'cept you wouldn't make it 'fore you freeze t'death. Gettin' purty cold at night these days."

Arvid got up from the table, probably thinking that he still might get pressured into having a cup of the malignant brew residing in the coffee pot. "Say, Smoked-Ham, if we could get that bucksaw..."

"Yeah, come on out to the woodshed an' pick one out."

I started walking to the door and abruptly recoiled. I had almost stepped on a four-foot snake lying just inside the open doorway.

Disapprovingly, Smoked-Ham looked down at the snake. "You in the house again? Git tha hell outta here!" He expertly stuck the toe of his boot under the snake and lofted it out the door. "He likes t'come inside when the weather turns cold. But I don't think a snake has any bizness in the house, do you?" I shook my head.

Arvid picked out a bucksaw, and we were starting to leave when I had to find out something.

"Ummm...whaddaya feed all those dogs?"

"Anythin' they kin catch."

I hurried after Arvid.

We hiked back to the command car, and in five minutes Arvid had cut the stump off and we were on our way again. We got to the camp about noon. Compared to Smoked-Ham's place, Arvid's camp looked like something out of Better Homes and Gardens. The door and window sills sparkled with fresh white paint, and the tar paper on the roof was a bright shade of green.

But when I looked at Arvid, I knew something was wrong. He was staring intently at one corner of the log cabin, and the muscles in his jaw were bulging. He got out of the command car, strode over to the cabin, and knelt down at the corner of the building. When I came up, I immediately saw what the problem was.

Something had been gnawing at the logs that made up the cabin walls. The bark had been chewed away in several spots.

"What did that?" I asked.

"Porcupine. They eat bark."

"But, why would he want to eat the camp? The woods is full of trees!"

"They like the salt from your hands. They'll always go for a log that some-body's handled."

"So, what are ya goin' t'do?"

"He'll be back. An' then I'll shoot 'im!"

We unpacked the command car and spent the rest of the afternoon walking the road, looking for partridge, with no luck. Arvid cooked up an elegant supper of pork and beans, fried potatoes, hardtack, and coffee. I had the foresight to bring some jelly roll for dessert. Around eight-thirty we got ready for bed. The last thing Arvid did before he put out the kerosene lamp was to place his revolver on a small night stand next to his bed.

CRUNCH...CRUNCH...CRUNCH...CRUNCH

I woke up, with a start, in inky blackness. For several seconds I couldn't remember where I was, but then I heard Arvid muttering and getting out of bed, over to my right, and it all came back.

The porcupine! He was out there eating the cabin!

Inside the cabin, I heard Arvid go across the room and then—SMACK—flesh struck wood. Something metal hit the wooden floor and went rolling to a wall.

"Aghh...dammit!"

THUMP...THUMP...THUMP...

What the hell's going on? A cold whiff of air hit me as the door opened.

BLLAAMMM!!! BLLAAMMM!!! BLLAAMMM!!!

The muzzle flashes from the revolver outlined Arvid standing just outside the door in his long underwear, pointing the revolver at the corner where the porcupine had been chewing.

Silence and darkness. A kitchen match ignited and Arvid lit the kerosene lamp. I figured that Arvid had been reaching for the flashlight in the dark when he stubbed his toe on the table leg. The flashlight had fallen on the floor and rolled under the table. The gunshots were his best guess where the porcupine was.

I flopped my legs over the edge of the bed onto the floor. "Did'ja get 'im?"

Arvid was rubbing his big toe. "I dunno. Prob'ly not. Black as hell out there."

We put on clothes and went out with the flashlight, but the porcupine was nowhere to be seen. There was no moon, and the sky was still overcast so the night was a black, velvet cloak.

The next morning we inspected the outside of the cabin. While there wasn't much danger of the porcupine doing serious structural damage anytime soon, it was an insult to Arvid's craftsmanship. Gawd, I hated that porcupine! Maybe I'd get him in the sights of my twenty-gauge today and I could bring him over to Mushrat Rommi to make porcupine stew!

Arvid took it philosophically. "He'll be back 'cause that's the way they are. He ain't smart an' he ain't fast. I'll get 'im next time."

We spent the morning bird hunting, but again, had no luck. Arvid wanted to do some chores around the camp in the afternoon so I went out alone. I discovered another abandoned logging road running south and proceeded down it in a last-ditch effort to at least get a shot at a partridge before the weekend was over. I had gone about a mile when...

FLUBFLUBFLUBFLUBFLUB

A partridge! He had been standing in one of the road ruts about thirty feet in front of me when he took to the air. I was so startled that he had ducked into the trees before I even got the shotgun up to my shoulder. But, after squatting down and looking beneath the tree limbs, I saw him land again! I cocked the hammer on the twenty-gauge and stepped into the trees, never taking my eyes off the partridge. He stood there for a few seconds and then strutted slowly away from me. I slowly put the shotgun up to my shoulder and continued to creep forward, waiting for him to step into a clear spot so I could get a shot. There he was! I could see him clearly!

BLLLAAAMMM!!!!!!

He flew further into the trees. Damn! I had cranked off the shot before I had taken good aim. I broke into a run to keep him in sight. I caught a glimpse of him running through a patch of young spruce trees which didn't offer him much cover. But suddenly the ground became dense with ferns, and I lost sight of him. I broke into a faster run to the point where I had seen him last, to see if I could flush him again, but nothing happened.

I stopped and just stood there, gasping for breath, listening for any sound of him—but the woods were silent.

Gawd, I hated to lose that bird! It was the only one I had seen in two days! But, maybe he had a couple of friends back at the road. I decided to go back and continue my patrol of the logging road.

I had turned around and started back, muttering to myself, when I entered a stand of birch trees. I stopped. Did I just go through these birch trees? I didn't remember them. But I was really busy chasing the bird and I could have. Still and all, birch trees are hard to miss with the white bark. I stopped again and took a good look in all directions.

Nothing looked familiar.

A tinge of anxiety crept into my head. Wait a minute! Get a grip here! How about that patch of young spruce trees that the partridge had run into just after I had taken my shot? That wasn't too far off the road! All I had to do was find the spruce trees, and I was all right! I broke off into a trot in one direction. After about a minute or so, not seeing any young spruce, I veered off to my left to try a different direction. Another minute went by, and I stopped for breath. I was getting a curious tightening in my throat, and my heart was rapping away in my chest. I looked around at the trees. Jack pine, spruce, maple, poplar, birch...these were all trees that I had seen all my life, but now they stood there with their branches upraised, closing in on me!

I yanked out my Bulova pocket watch. Quarter to three. In a couple of hours it was going to be dark. Then I remembered the blackness from last night!

Jezzzusssss!!!...I know! I'll fire a shot and Arvid will hear it! I pointed the shotgun into the air, cocked the hammer, and fired.

BLLLAAAMMM!!!!!

The blast split an otherwise dead landscape. Wait a minute! What the hell am I doing? He'll just think I'm shooting at partridge! That is, if he hears it at all!

I didn't have the foggiest idea how far from camp I was. I knew that I had walked quite a way early in the afternoon. But what direction is the camp? The words of Smoked-Ham popped into my brain:

"IF YOU PICK THE WRONG DIRECTION, YOU COULD
KEEP WALKIN' TILL YOU GET TO CRYSTAL FALLS, 'CEPT
YOU WOULDN'T MAKE IT 'FORE YOU FREEZE T'DEATH."

I let out a ragged gasp and took off at a dead run. Branches whipped at my face, and one of them snatched my woolen cap from my head. I stopped abruptly to get the cap and slid on wet leaves, falling on my butt. The twenty-gauge went flying into some ferns. I lay there gasping and moaning.

Then I remembered something my old man had told me a few years back. He said, "If you get lost in the woods an' you find yourself running, then you're doin' yourself no good at all. Sit down an' jus' listen awhile. Sooner or later, you're bound to hear somethin'."

I got up, retrieved my cap and the shotgun, and looked around for a place to sit. There was a granite outcropping which looked to be drier than the ground, so I went over and sat. I was still far from calm, but my mind was starting to function again. I took my supply of shotgun shells from the pocket of my mackinaw and counted them. When it got dark, Arvid was bound to figure something was wrong and I would fire the shotgun at intervals. He'd probably do the same thing, and with luck, we could find each other. But, gawdamm! Doin' that in pitch-black darkness wasn't pleasant to contemplate!

I heard something rustling in the leaves.

I grabbed the shotgun but didn't cock the hammer since I was hoping and praying that it was a person and not an animal. It was approaching from my right, and I could see the ferns moving. It was too small to be human.

It was a porcupine!

Is that the one that's been eating Arvid's camp? Might be! Just to be on the safe side I'll let him have it. I cocked the hammer of the shotgun and aimed. He was only about ten yards away and was proceeding along at his usual, leisurely, porcupine waddle. I couldn't miss.

Maybe...just maybe...he was going to Arvid's camp...

Then, I uncocked the hammer and put the shotgun down.

Maybe...just maybe...he was going to Arvid's camp for his evening chow.

I watched him, and he was definitely not just foraging for food but appeared to have a particular destination in mind. I fell in behind him, and we moved out at a sedate half mile an hour.

Have I gone completely nuts? The woods are full of porcupines, and even if it was the same one, it was much too early for him to be going to the camp. Last night it was in the middle of the night when he started chewing on the cabin. Maybe he's going to see his girl friend before he eats. Maybe the revolver shots scared him off for good. Maybe he's going to visit relatives in Crystal Falls and wasn't due to arrive until next summer... What if my friends found out that I got lost in the woods and latched on to a strange porcupine, to whom I hadn't even been introduced, to act as navigator to lead me to safety?

On the other hand, how much more lost could I get if I follow him till dark? He's going so damn slow that I wouldn't be that much further away from the camp than I am now.

So, for the next hour or so, I followed this walking pincushion. We were coming up a gentle slope when I looked up through the tops of the trees.

Smoke. I could see smoke!

Then I heard an axe splitting wood.

My heart started hammering in my chest again, and I dashed past the porcupine to the top of the slope.

There, about a hundred yards away, was Arvid's camp with smoke trailing out of the stovepipe in the roof. Arvid was chopping firewood by the front door.

The revolver was strapped to his waist.

I turned around and the stupid porcupine was still coming!

I walked back to him, and he stopped when I got within ten feet. I spoke to him in a loud whisper.

"Hey, Porky! Get outta here! You wanna get filled with lead? Shoo...shoo! Go find someone else's camp to chew on!"

He just stood there with his head bobbing from left to right, waiting for the obstacle to move, his opaque, beady eyes looking at my boots.

Arvid was right. He wasn't too smart, and he certainly wasn't very fast. On the other hand, he wasn't the one who had been lost in the woods, and he had gotten me here before dark. But, if I didn't do something, he was going to die! I raised my twenty-gauge, cocked the hammer, and fired.

BLLLAAAMMM!!!!

The dead leaves exploded about five feet from the porcupine's nose. He jumped and scurried off to the right. That was as quick as I had seen him move all afternoon.

I walked up to the camp, and Arvid was standing there with the axe in his hand.

"You must'a flushed a bird up there, huh?"

"Yeah, but there was too much brush for a good shot."

"I wuz startin' to wonder about you. It's gonna be dark pretty soon."

"Oh...I was OK. Jus' not too many birds around here this season."

"Well, we better have an early supper. We gotta long drive back, an' you got school tomorrow."

While Arvid was concocting another delicious repast of fried Spam and potatoes, I casually walked outside, grabbed a couple pieces of firewood, and walked into the woods where I had last seen the porcupine. I rubbed my hands all over the wood and, for good measure, took the salt shaker that I had filched from the camp table out of my pocket, and sprinkled the firewood liberally with salt. I threw the wood on the ground.

"Now, fer cryin' out loud, stay the hell away from the camp!"

I turned and went back to have supper.

What was the chances of all of that happening like it did? About six million to one. Like I said, I'm convinced God really has a sense of humor.

Appleknocker Season

*A*n' jus' where in the hell d'ya think I'm gonna get thirty-five dollars from?" This was the old man's stock rhetorical question for any financial issues that involved outflow of capital. He poured coffee through the strainer into one of our matched set of chipped Woolworth coffee cups.

The question had torpedoed me on past occasions, but this time I was prepared. I carefully folded the upper corner of the page displaying the Winchester 30-30 carbine hunting rifle in our brand new 1949 Sears, Roebuck catalog and turned to the Time Payment section in the back.

I launched into my counterattack without delay. "There's another way. We just send 'em four dollars, and they send the rifle."

The old man placed two cubes of sugar on his tongue in preparation for his first of many cups of coffee for the day. I tried to catch him early because his mind grew razor-sharp once he had a couple of cups under his belt.

"Oh? An' why would they send you the rifle fer only four dollars?"

"Well, it really costs more than that, but that's all you have to send 'em at first."

"So you send 'em four dollars, an' they send you the rifle. Then what?"

"Well, you send 'em a little money each month. Not much though."

"How much is 'not much'?" He moved in like a trial lawyer, and my palms got clammy.

"Uh...four dollars a month."

"Fer how long?"

"Uh...a year, I think."

The old man slowly put down his coffee cup on the kitchen table oilcloth. He dropped his jaw so that his mouth hung open, and puckered his eyebrows in an expression of incomprehension. This was a look that he had refined over the years and reserved for occasions when he had just heard pure, unadulterated BS.

"A year? That's forty-eight dollars fer a thirty-five-dollar rifle! Why the hell would you wanna do that?"

"Because you don't have thirty-five dollars an' I don't have thirty-five dollars an' deer season is only a month off an' I don't have a rifle!"

Desperate times called for desperate measures, like plopping reality out on the table. This was the first year that I was old enough to get a deer-hunting license, and I had already contracted a raging case of buck fever. For several weeks I had been waking up, looking at the wall opposite my bed, and picturing the mounted head of a two-hundred-and-fifty-pound, sixteen-point buck. Then, I would hear the sizzle and smell the gamy aroma of a venison steak in the frying pan, as my mother prepared breakfast. We would live off that deer meat all winter. Of course, there would be the usual picture and article in *The Marquette Daily Mining Journal*, which appeared whenever a record buck was shot.

The old man had poured some coffee into the saucer to cool it down.

"You shoulda thought a that rifle last year if you wanna go huntin' this year! You coulda saved up fer it!"

Buying things on credit ranked up there with the Theory of Relativity to the old man. He would never understand either one of them. He operated on a strict cash-and-carry basis. If you wanted something badly enough, you simply saved your money until you could pay for it. After he and my mother were married they worked at various lumber camps in the woods of Upper Michigan. One day, after several years of pulp cutting and fighting mosquitoes, he counted the money they had saved and said to my mother: "I'm tired a livin' in the woods. What'dya say we go buy a house in town?" So, they found a house they liked, took out a roll of twenties, tens, fives, and ones and picked up the deed right on the spot. Buy a rifle on time? He kept looking at me like I didn't have both oars in the water.

I thumbed back to the catalog page with the 30-30 carbine on it and blinked back a tear. A fifteen-year-old male in Upper Michigan without a deer rifle was emasculation personified. Your ex-friends would talk about you in hushed tones. No self-respecting girl would be seen with you. Dogs would pee on your leg if you stood still.

My imminent emotional breakdown must have penetrated the crust on the old man's heart because he started to tug on his left ear lobe, which was a sign that he was giving the issue some deep thought. He got up from the table and walked into his bedroom, returning a minute later carrying a long weather-beaten khaki bag with a shoulder strap.

My one and only encounter with that bag occurred about ten years earlier during a covert adventure in my parents' bedroom to check out all of their mysterious adult stuff. I was quickly apprehended before I even got the bag open. All charges were eventually dismissed, but the old man made it crystal clear that if I ever touched the khaki bag again, he would personally rip off my butt. Since he was usually not given to idle threats, I didn't go near the bag again and, eventually, lost interest in it. So, I still didn't have the foggiest idea what was in it. The old man undid two cracked leather straps from metal buckles and opened up the bag.

What emerged, in two pieces, was the most disreputable-looking firearm I had ever seen. The butt stock was dull and bore so many scars that it appeared to have been used for fending off wild bear. The barrel was unusually long, hexagonal in cross section, and streaked with rust. It would have looked like a piece from the Spanish-American War except for the incongruity of a sliding wood handgrip attached to a cylindrical magazine underneath the barrel. It was a pump-action gun.

The old man assembled it quickly, put it up to his shoulder, sighted it at the center of the kitchen window, and pumped it twice.

"What is it? A 410 shotgun?" I asked.

"No! Fer chrissake! Why would I bring out a 410 shotgun when we're talkin' about deer season? It's a rifle!"

"I've never seen a pump-action rifle before."

"Yeah. Well, it's kinda old an' they don't make 'em like this anymore, I don't think. But, it's better'n payin' forty-eight dollars fer a thirty-five-dollar rifle."

"You mean you're gonna let me use it for deer season?"

"I'm gonna give it to ya. I don't figure to use it any more."

I didn't know whether to thank him, laugh, or cry. I was in the midst of several skirmishes with puberty, and one of the major engagements was "being one of the boys." For deer hunting, this limited your choice of weapons: the 30-30 carbine that I lusted after or a bolt-action repeater. The old man's rifle didn't faintly resemble either one of them. I was doomed to a solitary season of hunting, lest I make a spectacle of myself with this monstrosity. I'd have to go so far out in the bush that even the deer wouldn't know how to get there.

"Why's the barrel so long?" I said, thinking that the judicious use of a hacksaw would make it look a little sportier.

The old man gave me a withering look. "I kin see you don't know much about rifles. A longer barrel makes the slug go straighter. This gun'll outshoot that carbine you want any day."

I almost choked on that. First of all, I'd be lucky if the damn thing didn't blow up in my face, and if it did work, the slug would probably come out of the barrel end over end.

He reached into the khaki bag and pulled out a cleaning kit and a cartridge. "I'll clean up the inside of the barrel and oil 'er up, but I only got this one cartridge an' it'll be up to you to get some more."

I took the cartridge in my hand and looked at it. It was a rifle cartridge all right, but it looked different. "What kind is this?"

"It's a 32 Remington rimless. It looks different cause it don't have that rim on the back a the casing like a 30-30 cartridge. You better get started lookin' for 'em cause they might be hard to find. I ain't seen any in a long time."

Terrific. I was now the proud owner of a strange-looking gun that shoots strange bullets.

"Uh, Pop...how old is this rifle?"

"Well...I bought 'er in 1918 when I got outta the Army."

"So, it's 30 years old?"

"Older. I bought it used."

"When's the last time you fired it?"

"1926."

Terrific.

"Hmmmmm...Where dija get this?" Clem Hooper, our local arms dealer, fingered the cartridge and gazed at it through his bifocals with the scientific curiosity of an archaeologist handed a rare Egyptian artifact. Clem ran a combination hardware and sporting goods establishment in town and was the undisputed expert on guns and ammunition.

"I got it from my ol...it's for my new hunting rifle. It's an unusual cartridge, isn't it?"

"I never seen one before. For your new rifle, you say?"

"Yeah. It might be foreign ammunition or something."

"No...no...it ain't foreign. See—it says Remington right here on the bottom of the casing. But it ain't got a rim. Be gawdammed."

I put out my hand for the cartridge. "You know where I might find some of these?"

"Sure as hell don't. You might try Nyquist's in Marquette. They got more stock than I do."

In the two weeks that followed, that cartridge changed hands more times than a nude picture of Betty Grable. Since I didn't have a car, I had to give it to people who were driving to the neighboring towns and were willing to check out the sporting goods stores for me. As each day passed, I became more and more agitated. Deer season was going to start, and I had one bullet.

But, one night there was a knock on the kitchen door. My uncle Hugo, the current custodian of the cartridge, came in and threw a ragged-looking box on the kitchen table.

"Here ya are! A box of twenty 32 Remington rimless cartridges!"

I was saved! I picked up the box lovingly with both hands. "Hugo, how much do I owe you?"

"Six dollars. I hadda buy 'em from an ammo collector in Munising."

"Six dollars?" A box of fifty 22 shells cost fifty cents!

"Pay 'im an shut up!" the old man advised.

It was unquestionably a sellers' market. I went into my bedroom, dug into my life savings and gave Hugo six one-dollar bills.

"Now we gotta do some target practice," the old man said.

At thirty cents a shot! Terrific.

After I got out of school the following afternoon, the old man and I trudged up to an abandoned gravel quarry about a half mile from the house. He carried a large piece of cardboard with a white circle one-foot in diameter painted in the middle. I lugged the 275-pound rifle and the gold-plated bullets. He produced some white string and tied the cardboard target to some tree roots sticking out of a vertical sandy wall in the quarry.

"Aren't you going to put a smaller bull's-eye in the center of that circle?"

He smiled. "Let's see how we do with tha big circle first. You kin get fancy later on if you want."

We walked back about one hundred and fifty yards, and the old man pointed to a small mound in the dirt. "Here's a good place to lay prone an' try 'er."

I glanced at the target, and indeed, the one-foot circle looked a lot smaller than it did a minute ago. I gave him the box of cartridges, and he loaded up the six-shot magazine underneath the barrel. He got down on his stomach with his chest resting on the mound of dirt and his elbows in front of it. He aimed the rifle at the target.

"Wait a minute, Pop. Ain't I supposed to be the one that gets the target practice?"

He looked up at me. "You know anything about sightin' in a rifle?"

I shook my head. "Uh...nope."

"Then keep quiet fer awhile an you might learn somethin'." He pumped the rifle once to get a cartridge into the chamber and took aim at the target.

KAAA...POWWWWWWWW!!!!!!

For a few seconds I lost my hearing. I had been around when 30-30's had been fired, and they had a flat, nasty crack, but this thing sounded like the wrath of God.

A puff of sand appeared about two feet from the left edge of the cardboard. Damn! I knew this gun wasn't going to work!

The old man took a pair of dime store reading glasses from his shirt pocket, pulled a small screwdriver from somewhere in his pants, and loosened up the rear sight on the rifle. He tapped it a couple of times with the butt end of the screwdriver and tightened it back up. Again, he took aim at the target.

KAAA...POWWWWWWWW!!!!!!

This time the sand flew up about six inches from the right edge of the cardboard. We had just spent sixty cents and hadn't hit the target yet. Again, he put on his glasses, took out the screwdriver, and loosened up the rear sight. Then he gave it one light tap and tightened it back up.

KAAA...POWWWWWWWW!!!!!!

This time we didn't see any sand fly up at all.
"D'ya think you hit the cardboard?"
"Dunno. Let's go have a look."
We walked down to the target. The third slug had actually hit the white circle about four inches to the right of dead center. I was impressed.
The old man looked at the hole and scratched his chin. "Well...that's about as good as we're gonna get with that old iron sight. Jus' remember that she'll be pullin' a little to the right." We walked back to the mound.
I thought he was going to give me the gun then, but he jacked another shell into the chamber and, from a standing position, slapped the rifle up to his shoulder.

KAAA...POWWWWWWW!!!!!!
KAAA...POWWWWWWW!!!!!!
KAAA...POWWWWWWW!!!!!!

In less than two seconds he had cranked off three shots! I didn't think I was ever going to get my hearing back, but I found myself running down to the target in a state of high excitement. All three slugs had hit the circle within three inches of the center! My gawd! He could outshoot Sergeant York! Was he a secret weapon that we had used to win World War I?
The old man strolled up with the rifle in one hand. He glanced at the target and then turned to me. "Still think that carbine's the better gun, boy?" He figured that I deserved that ninety-cent lesson.
We walked back up to the mound and he handed me the rifle. "OK, it's your turn."
I froze up! I would never be able to shoot like that, and besides, I had only fifteen cartridges left, with no hope of getting any more!
"Uhhh...I think you got her sighted in pretty good, Pop. I don't think we have to use up any more ammo today."

"It only takes one good shot to bring down a buck, an' you ain't takin' that rifle outta the house unless I know that you can hit what yer shootin' at!"

Twenty minutes later we walked back to the house, and I was now down to nine cartridges. My ears were ringing, and there was a strong possibility that a doctor would need to reset my shoulder. The only thing that saved the rest of my precious ammunition was that my sixth shot had hit the circle an inch from the edge. Letting me off easy, the old man said that he thought I was getting the hang of it, but I think that if I got a report card in marksmanship, it would have been no better than a C minus.

"Gawdamm! Whatizatt? An old 410 shotgun?" My pal Carl Kettu had a smirky grin on his face as he looked at my rifle. It was six o'clock Saturday morning and the first day of deer-hunting season. I had opted to risk the ridicule from my peers and go out with Carl, for the simple reason that he had a driver's license and his old man's 1936 Ford. If I was going to get that sixteen-point buck for my wall, I needed all the range and mobility that I could muster.

I had worked diligently on the rifle's appearance over the last few evenings, using steel wool and oil on the barrel, and liberal quantities of a linseed oil and turpentine mixture on the scars and scratches in the stock. But, this was the Quasimodo of rifles, and nothing was going to make it look like Tyrone Power.

"This is a 32 Remington pump action, and it's been in my family for years!"

"Oh, yeah? The stock looks like yer old man clubbed the bucks over the head to save on ammo!"

"Lisssen! This gun will outshoot your carbine any time!"

"Hah! That'll be the day! That barrel's so long, I dunno if we can get it in the car. Don't poke a hole in the roof now."

I knew that if I could get through the first ten minutes of jibes, we could get down to some serious deer hunting. "Where'll we go this morning?"

Carl gave me a crafty grin. "I figure we'll go out the east road about ten miles or so an' see what's happenin'."

"But...that's appleknocker country!"

"I know. But we'll let the appleknockers scare up the bucks, an' we can sit on a rock an' pick 'em off!"

You see, every year during early November, Michigan's sleepy, remote, and usually forgotten Upper Peninsula experienced a phenomenon which was blessed by a few and cursed by most—the influx of deer hunters from Lower Michigan, Wisconsin, Illinois, Ohio, Indiana, and other points south. These were the appleknockers, and they came by land and sea. They roared up from Green Bay,

Milwaukee, and Chicago, and they steamed across the Straits of Mackinac on ferry boats which provided the link between the Lower and Upper Peninsulas. During the 1950's the State of Michigan saw fit to abet the invasion by building them the longest suspension bridge in the world across the Straits.

No one knows exactly how they got the appleknocker label. Sources of American slang define an appleknocker as a bumpkin or a migratory fruit picker, but these people didn't fit either of those profiles, whatsoever. They were relatively affluent and, as far as anybody knew, didn't have any use for fruit, except as a possible adornment for mixed drinks. Whiskeyknockers would have been closer to the mark.

And so they came, in their station wagons, Cadillacs, Lincolns, and Chryslers; gaily decked out in stylish red plumage from pricey sporting goods shops; and often carrying European hand-engraved rifles. Appleknockers were easy to spot because they made the local denizens look like ragpickers.

While some were serious and experienced hunters, most appleknockers arrived in groups of three on up, bent on a two-week stag party away from the little woman. Male bonding combined with loaded guns and booze made a particularly lethal combination. While most locals gave them a wide berth in the woods, hardly a season went by when some dentist from Detroit didn't receive the ultimate cavity, being mistaken for a big twelve-point buck by one of his peers.

Farmers and pet owners hated them passionately. Cows were known to have gone to an early reward with the words

"I AM A COW"

printed in large letters across their ribs. Normally footloose dogs were kept securely tied to the house during the two weeks of deer season.

So why was this band of pickled marauders tolerated every November? Economics. The Upper Peninsula of Michigan has been on the brink of hard times ever since they discovered a better grade of iron ore in Minnesota, and the bucks that the appleknockers brought in more than made up for the relatively few bucks that they took out on the fenders of their cars. Liquor stores, hotels, and anyone with a cabin to rent made out like bandits. Another interesting, but subterranean, business was the buck that was shot with the "silver bullet." Some natives who bagged a buck would wait awhile before putting their tag on the antlers to see if it would fetch a steep price from some desperate appleknocker who needed it to convince the wife that he really was out in the woods for the last two weeks.

But, everybody who had an ounce of sense agreed on one basic rule. Don't go near them in the woods. And so, Carl and I sped toward the early morning dawn, on the first day of deer season, looking for the largest nest of appleknockers that we could find.

The sky streaked with gray light through the windshield as we drove along the ever-narrowing east road through an area of small lakes where the appleknockers rented cabins.

"I brought a box a shells. How 'bout you?"

"Nah," I said, getting an early morning energy blast with a Mounds bar and black coffee that I had brought along in a thermos. "It only takes one good shot to bring down a buck. I brought about eight or nine. I dunno. I didn't count 'em."

Carl slowed the car abruptly. "Look! There's a coupla them ahead!"

In the headlights we saw a parked station wagon with the tailgate down, and two hunters with matching red vests had just taken out a washtub filled with a chopped-up block of ice and about a half a case of beer. They squinted at us as they crossed the road carrying the washtub between them with their rifles in the other hand.

"Damn!" Carl exclaimed, "Those buggers really know to put 'em away, don't they? I sure could use wunna them beers right now."

"Yeah!" I agreed. "A cuppla beers would get the season started off just right."

"Y'know? I betcha if we followed those two into the bush, we could see where they put the tub down, an' when they go off lookin' for deer we could help ourselves to the beer."

"I dunno. I don't think it's a good idea to get too close to 'em. They might hear us an' think we're a buck an' take a shot at us." In fact, the old man had told me to stay the hell away from this area.

"Hell! I could walk around 'em all day long an' they'd never hear me! Well, let's keep this place in mind and see what's up ahead." Carl sped up the Ford, and we left the station wagon behind.

It got light quickly, and we started seeing many more parked cars along the road, several with Wisconsin and Illinois license plates. Carl turned left onto an abandoned logging road, which was now nothing more than a two-rut cleared path through the spruce and pines.

"I came up here during bird season, an' there's a big clearing 'bout a quarter mile in. I figure we can find a place on the edge an' pick off a buck or two that the appleknockers chase through."

We got to the clearing, parked the car, and set up shop in a rock outcropping on the edge of the clearing. But, it soon became apparent that we weren't alone. As the sun filtered through the trees, voices drifted across the clearing.

"Ralph? Where you at? I gotta get the keys to the car."

"Over here! When you go back to the car, get the other bottle opener. I dropped the gawdamm thing in these ferns an can't find it!"

"Hey, Nick! Jimmy over here. Bring back some a those Twinkies an' a coupla more bottles a beer."

"Did anybody bring any toilet paper? I gotta take a crap sumthin' awful!"

"Whattya think the ferns are for? Hahahahaha!"

Carl looked at me and slowly shook his head. "Didja ever hear anything like that in your life? A buck'd hafta be deaf, dumb, an' blind to be shot by that bunch."

We started to hear sporadic rifle fire in the distance. Suddenly a shot rang out nearby. We both checked the safety on our rifles.

"Hey, Nick! You think there's one comin' our way?"

"I'm ready for 'im!"

More shots at close range.

Rrrrruuuuppppppp!!!!!—sounded over my head like someone quickly ripping a piece of cardboard in half.

I turned to Carl. "What was that?"

He gave me a toothy grin. "That was a 30-30 slug, man. What'ja think it was? A fast bird passin' gas? Heh, heh, heh."

"Well...I knew what it was. I jus' never heard one that close up."

"Hey, we never flipped to see who's gonna get first shot."

I fumbled in my pants pocket. "You wanna flip?"

Carl gave a magnanimous wave of his hand. "Nah. This's my second season, an' it's only your first. You kin have first shot."

Rrrrruuuupppppppp!!!!!

I crouched lower between two rocks, but Carl was enjoying it to the hilt. "Gawddd! Lissen to those babies hum over!"

Suddenly a flash of brown with a white tail burst into the clearing—a buck! I put the rifle up, but it was jinking across the clearing at a furious rate. The thought of thirty cents a shot flashed into my mind. Was it a buck or a doe? I couldn't even see the head clearly, much less any antlers. Either the appleknockers had much better eyesight than I did, or they weren't troubled with legal issues, because rifle fire erupted all around the clearing. The deer disappeared into the trees. It was all over in three seconds.

Carl was steamed. "Why didncha shoot? I coulda got 'im easy! Jeeesus!"

The Lone Ranger couldn't have hit that deer, much less me or the appleknockers.

"Aaww...it wasn't a very good shot. I may only have wounded 'im if I had tried it, an' I hate to chase a wounded buck through the bush."

We sat in the rocks for the next hour or so, listening to intermittent rifle fire and an occasional Rrrrruuuupppppp!!!!! overhead. The passing slugs had put Carl back into a mellow frame of mind.

"Maybe we outta go back an' look fer those two with the washtub a beer. I'm sure gettin' thirsty!"

My stomach was starting to growl. My coffee was gone and I was hoarding the last half of my Mounds bar. "Yeah, well it sounds like a goo..."

Just then we both heard a metallic ping behind us followed by a shot. We looked at each other, and neither of us said anything. The '36 Ford had just taken a slug.

Carl scrambled to his feet and ran over to the car. A neat bullet hole was right in the center of the left rear door. The color of the car was light brown, and I suppose, to a well-oiled appleknocker, it may have looked like a very fat deer wearing eyeglasses.

"Gawd allmighty! Some stupid appleknocker shot my car!"

"Look, Carl, just tell your old man exactly what happened and that it was an accident. What can he say?"

"What can he say? He'll know I been out here, an he'll kick my ass to hell and back!" He ran back to the edge of the clearing.

"HEY, YOU DUMB BASTARDS! DOES A '36 FORD LOOK LIKE A BUCK TO YOU?"

"Who tha hell's that, Ralph?"

"I dunno. Sounds like some snot-nosed local yokel ta me. WATCH THAT MOUTH OF YOURS, SONNY! I STILL GOT PLENTY OF AMMO LEFT!"

I ran up to Carl and grabbed his jacket. "Hey, let's get outta here! Those guys are so sloshed on beer that there's no tellin' what they'll do."

Carl walked stiff-legged back to the car and we drove out to the main road. We got out and inspected the Ford. The bullet had passed through the door and had disappeared into the bottom cushion of the rear seat.

Carl completely forgot about hunting and focussed on damage control. "Ya know? If I can get some putty in the shop at school I think I can patch up this hole real good. Finding a color of brown close to this should be easy." Carl gave me his trademark foxy grin. "I can fix 'er up so's the old man'll never know!"

He dropped me off late in the morning, and I walked into the kitchen just as the old man was starting in on his fifth cup of coffee.

"So, yer back early. Any luck?"

"Nope."

"Where'd ya go?"

I found out a long time ago that it didn't pay to lie to him. "Out east."

"I thought I tol' you not to go out there!"

"I know, but that's where Carl wanted to go, an' he was driving."

"He's damn lucky one of those crazy bastards didn't shoot his car. Lissen, you wanna know where to get yer buck this year?"

"Sure!"

"Well, we'll hike out to the cemetery tomorrow mornin' an' I'll show you somthin'."

The next morning we walked about a mile to the town cemetery next to my grandmother's house. The weather was turning colder, but we still didn't have any snow on the ground. We walked about halfway in, and the old man stopped and pointed to soft earth next to the asphalt road.

"The last coupla mornings, after I drop off yer grandmother's mail, I been walkin' in here an' lookin' around. That's gotta be a ten or twelve-point buck that crosses through here regular."

I looked down and, sure enough, there were fresh tracks of a very large deer. A little further up there were more tracks, not so fresh, but apparently the same deer.

The old man continued. "As near as I kin figure, he comes from that cedar swamp over there and passes through here just after sunup. As soon as we start to get some snow, someone'll spot these tracks fer sure an' the place'll be crawlin' with hunters!"

He pointed over to an outcropping of rocks and underbrush in the middle of the cemetery.

"If you were over there waitin' fer him tomorrow mornin' at dawn, I think you'd stand a pretty good chance a nailin' him!"

I felt like giving him a hug, but he wasn't through with the briefing.

"Now, yer gonna hafta remember two things. You get in those rocks an' don't move around. An' if the wind is blowin' from where yer at to where he comes from, he'll smell you an' you might as well pack up an' go home."

The next morning, well before sunup, I trudged over to the cemetery and deposited myself in the rock outcropping. Fumbling around in a dark cemetery wasn't exactly my idea of a fun pastime, but the sure-fire expectation of bagging this buck eclipsed any fears of the supernatural. The weather was even colder than the day before. It was one of those late autumn Upper Peninsula days where the temperature suddenly dives well below freezing, and you're caught without the winter viscosity in your blood. Besides, my mother hadn't yet forced me to drag out the six tons of winter clothing that I would lug around on my back for the next four months. I didn't have on any long underwear, a cap with ear flaps, or gloves.

So, I waited as the dim morning light slowly gave definition to the tombstones. As I huddled there, turning blue, I made a permanent decision on cremation since I sure as hell didn't want to spend an eternity of winters planted in this boneyard.

An hour went by, and the buck of my dreams failed to show. A wind had sprung up and sent icy spears up the back of my mackinaw. I inadvertently shifted my left hand to the metal magazine of the rifle, and it felt like a popsicle. Painful past experience induced me to check my ears and, sure enough, the tips were numb. I was on the verge of getting frostbite.

...the buck of my dreams failed to show...

Quickly, I laid down the rifle and started to rub both of my ears, not doing much good because both of my hands were now like blocks of ice. It suddenly occurred to me that if I was going to thaw out, I had to move, and if I moved, the buck was going to see me. But, it was well past sunup and he hadn't appeared yet—maybe he was sleeping in because of the weather. The hell with it! I picked up the rifle, stumbled out of the rocks, and walked the short distance over to my grandmother's house.

My grandmother had come over from Finland shortly after she got married, and I was one of her favorite grandchildren for the simple reason that I didn't talk too much, and spoke slowly when I did, providing her an excellent opportunity to practice her English. She always had a large pot of strong coffee on the wood stove supported by a monumental array of sugar-laden goodies that my raging case of acne currently required.

Forty-five minutes, two cups of coffee, and three jelly donuts later I felt fortified enough to have another go at the cemetery. I walked through the gate and looked at the now half-frozen earth that the old man had shown me the day before.

The buck had crossed through while I was having coffee.

I looked again to make sure that they weren't old tracks, but there wasn't any doubt. Fresh hoof marks had scarred the frost layer that wasn't there yesterday. If I had had enough sense to look out the window while I was slurping coffee, I could have dropped him with a well-placed shot from the kitchen door.

How was I going to break the news to the old man? He had practically shoved the rifle barrel into the buck's mouth for me, and I had blown it! Is everybody, including all of the wildlife in the woods, smarter than I am?

Heartbroken, I walked home. The old man was getting ready to leave as I walked in the back door.

"I expected you back long before now! With this north wind blowin' he was never gonna cross through the cemetery with you in those rocks. He'd smell you a mile off!"

The wind! I forgot! Everybody *was* smarter than me!

He must have sensed how I felt because he said, "Well, if it dies down tomorrow, you kin try it again. Jus' be patient. Yer luck'll change."

But my luck didn't change. During the next ten days the north wind held steady, and while I went up to the cemetery and saw his tracks every morning, I knew the big buck would just wait me out if I was in the rocks. I tried other places, before and after school, but didn't see a thing. Carl's old man had spotted the bullet hole in the '36 Ford and had grounded him indefinitely, so my range was limited.

With two days left of the season I had pretty much given up on the whole endeavor and was soothing my ego after school with a truly substantial investment into Mounds bars at the Red Owl store.

"Well, son, have you had any luck with deer hunting this season?"

I turned around from the counter and faced an appleknocker in full dress. He was waiting to pay for a quart of milk. I had never seen an appleknocker buy a bottle of milk before. He wore rimless glasses, which I had also never seen before, and sported a well-trimmed mustache. He looked like an actor who would play Cary Grant's lawyer.

"Nah, but I haven't had a chance to get out very much this year. I might go out tomorrow and bag one though."

"Tell me, I haven't seen a darned thing since the season started, and I have to leave tomorrow evening to drive back to Chicago. Do you know of anyone who could give me a tip on where I might find a nice buck to take a crack at? I would make it worth their while."

I gazed thoughtfully out of the store window at the Post Office across the street. The flag was still flying under the force of the north wind.

"I can show you where there's going to be a buck tomorrow morning. You got a car?"

He looked at me shrewdly for a few seconds. "Of course."

"Then let's go. It's not going to stay light too much longer."

He quickly paid for the milk and we left the store. He walked up to a royal blue 1949 Buick Roadmaster parked outside the store. The car looked like it had just been built last week, and it made the whole street look seedy by comparison. I swallowed a mouthful of saliva.

He unlocked the passenger side door as I fingered one of the shiny exhaust ports built into the front fender.

"Where are we going?" he said.

"I'll give you directions."

He started up the Buick and the V-8 engine purred obediently. We made a U-turn and headed for the cemetery, just as Carl Kettu came out of the four-lane bowling alley and spotted me in the car. His mouth hung open. I gave him a curt nod as we passed.

I breathed in the bouquet of the new car. I had never ridden in a new car before because I didn't know anyone who could afford one. I wanted to touch the dashboard but decided that it wouldn't appear very businesslike.

We got to the cemetery just as the daylight began to fade. I showed him the tracks and pointed to the rocks and brush in the center of the cemetery.

"He'll come along here just after sunup, and if you make yourself nice and cozy up there in the rocks, you can probably nail him."

He got a big smile on his face and started to bounce from one foot to the other. But, I wasn't through with the briefing.

"Now, you have to remember one thing. You have to stay very still in those rocks or else he'll see you."

He nodded his head vigorously. "But, tell me, son. How is it that you haven't taken him for yourself?"

"Well, it's only a sunup shot, and I usually get to school very early to work on a physics experiment that I'm involved in. I was thinking of taking some time off and coming out here tomorrow morning and getting him myself. However, since you've driven such a long way, he's yours if you want him. I'll just find another one tomorrow."

"My boy, it's gratifying to find such an expert woodsman in a person so young as yourself. How much do I owe you?"

"Uhh...six dollars."

"Of course! Of course!" He pulled out an alligator wallet and gave me a one and a five. "Six dollars is a rather odd amount. How did you arrive at it?"

"Ahh...I've had some unexpected expenses recently."

"I see. Tell me...I don't suppose that you carry business cards, do you?"

"What?"

He laughed. "I guess not. What I'm getting at is that I plan to come up here again next November, and I was thinking of hiring you on as a guide. Maybe I could just get your telephone number."

"Telephone?"

"Yes. I've got a pen and card of my own right here. I'll just write it down."

"Uhhh...I'm a little hard to get hold of by telephone, but I've got a special box number where I receive my mail. Why don't you just drop me a line next year."

"That would be just fine! Would fifty dollars for the two weeks be suitable?"

"Fifff..." I had never seen fifty dollars in one place.

"I realize that it might be a hardship since you're still in high school, but I'm sure that we can work out some kind of schedule."

"Oh yeah!!!" I said. A pang of guilt suddenly stabbed me. "You know? There is one more thing that I gotta tell you about tomorrow morning. If you're upwind of that buck, he may not come into the cemetery. I just thought you oughta know that."

A look of perplexity crossed his face momentarily, but he resumed his good humor. "I'll keep that in mind. Now, I'd better get back to the lodge that I leased. Tomorrow's going to be an early day."

We exchanged addresses, and he dropped me off at the house. I stared intently at the Roadmaster as the appleknocker drove off in the dusk, memorizing every detail of the design. With the income from my new enterprise, I could easily afford one of those in a couple of years. Blue was a nice color, but if I was going to be driving out in the woods every day during deer season, red would be more appropriate. I certainly didn't want any bullet holes in it. As a matter of fact, a convertible would be the most practical, affording the clients maximum visibility with the top down. Ah—yes! A red convertible, with my name on the door in gold letters. Below the name in smaller letters:

HUNTING GUIDE SERVICES.

I walked in just in time for supper. My mother was setting the table, and the old man was having his appetizer cup of coffee.

"Uh...Pop. What exactly are business cards?"

"What kinda cards?"

"Business cards."

"What kinda business?"

"Any kind of business, I guess."

"What in the hell are you talkin' about?"

"Uh...never mind. I just thought that I might need some business cards some day. Uh...when do you think that we might get a telephone?"

"He put his coffee cup down. "A telephone! Did that day in the rocks freeze your brain, boy? Where in tha hell d'ya think I'm gonna get money fer a telephone?"

My mother interrupted the discussion by plopping down steaming bowls of Finnish stew in front of us.

The old man looked at me. "Well, I guess maybe you don't get your buck this season, but next year'll come around soon enough."

My mother snorted. "I'm just glad that those appleknockers will be leaving! What a gang of drunks and roughnecks! I was worried about you every day when you were out in the woods."

I laid my spoon in the stew. "Well...I think that some of them are probably pretty decent people."

My mother snorted again. "I suppose that's right, once their wives sober them up!"

The old man carved up a boiled potato with his spoon. "Well, that big buck'll probably still be crossin' the cemetery every morning next November."

I nodded my head philosophically. "Yeah, I suppose so. But you know? There's more important things to consider in life besides shooting a deer."

The old man glanced over at me, trying to digest that weighty remark. A gust of wind from the north shook the storm windows in response.

Michigan Graffiti

A juvenile Harrison Ford peered out from under a straw cowboy hat and coolly appraised a brunette with Rose Queen qualifications as they sat in adjacent cars at the red light. He was behind the wheel of a mean, souped-up '57 Chevy and had just dumped a eye-popping blonde in order to carve another notch in his fender before the evening drew to a close. Without a word being spoken, she motioned to him that she was going to pull over past the light. She parked her car and jumped into his Chevy and they rumbled off down some unnamed boulevard in the San Fernando Valley.

I was watching *American Graffiti* on one of the cable channels, a true cinema classic in every sense of the word, that launched several people into later stardom. After thoroughly enjoying the movie up to that point, I now sipped moodily on my Diet Cherry Coke. The pickup scene had stretched my imagination beyond credulity. I mean, real life isn't like that! Ever since the wheel was invented, guys have been cruising around trying to pick up women, and it's a difficult, frustrating job which demands the utmost in masculine guile and ingenuity. For openers, most guys don't look like Harrison Ford, but, aside from that, there are still a thousand other factors, totally out of a guy's control, that stack the deck against him. I started to fantasize about plucking this cocky kid from my TV screen and time-warping him to Upper Michigan in the dead of winter in the late 1940's. Ah, yes...he would have been up against different odds...

I fished a red bandanna out of my hip pocket and wiped the condensation from the inside of the passenger side window. It was a Saturday night in late January 1949, and Carl Kettu and I were cruising around town in his old man's '41 Ford pickup truck. Carl had a four-month-old driver's license, and I was still three months shy of the legal age, so when it came to cruising, we were still in the novice class. But, the adrenaline and hormones were perking, and what we lacked in experience, we made up with enthusiasm and dedication. We patrolled the dimly lit streets with their hard-packed snow surfaces. The sixty-watt street lamps painted weird shadows on the huge snowbanks that covered the sidewalks.

I pointed to the Montgomery Ward heater, mounted under the dash, blasting a steady torrent of hot air into the cab. "Carl, I know it's five above zero out there, but do you have to have that thing going full blast?"

Carl was trying to roll a cigarette and steer at the same time, a skill which was very high on his life priorities right then. We veered perilously close to a snowbank before he pulled at the steering wheel. He stuck a very curious-looking, bloated cigarette in his mouth and took out a wooden match.

"The heater's part of my plan fer tonight."

"Plan?"

"Yeah. Think about it. On a cold night like this, alla the girls are gonna be bundled up good. How are ya gonna cop a good feel if you don't get 'em to take off their coats an' sweaters first?"

"Sounds like a good plan, but can't we wait till we get the girls before we turn it on? I took a shower an hour ago, an' in another half hour I'm gonna smell like a goat."

Carl had the wooden match in his right fist and scratched the match head with his thumb nail, a trick that Humphrey Bogart used to excellent advantage when he was lighting a woman's cigarette. However, Carl couldn't get it to ignite, and finally, in frustration, he scraped the match across the rusting metal dashboard of the truck. He put the lit match up to the hand-rolled cigarette, which immediately went up in a ball of flame. He spit it out on the floorboard and stamped on it with his boot.

"I think you better roll those cigarettes a lil' tighter, Carl, or you're gonna burn out all the hair in your nose."

"Shaddup, wiseguy...hey, look! There's a coupl'a girls up ahead."

I looked through the windshield at two huddled, walking figures silhouetted in the headlights against a giant snowbank by the Red Owl store.

As we got closer, I could see that they were wearing mackinaw jackets, pants, and boots and had woolen mufflers across their faces.

"They ain't girls, dummy. They're guys!"

"Like hell! Look at the mittens! They're wearing crocheted mittens! You know any guys that wear crocheted mittens?"

I peered closely as we passed them. All I could tell was that they were short and wearing crocheted mittens.

"You're right! Hey, they don't look too bad! Let's go around the block and ask 'em if they wanna ride."

Carl turned the corner by the Red Owl Store and dug into his coat pocket. He took out a Castoria bottle.

"You wanna belt before we pick 'em up?"

"Castoria? You gotta constipation problem?"

"Naw...it's Four Roses. I snuck it outta the old man's bottle before I left the house. It's easier to carry around like this." He took a nip from the bottle, scrunched up his eyes, and handed the bottle to me. My experience with drinking was about on a par with my experience at picking up girls, but I took a healthy slug.

The fumes that went up my nose got into a race with the molten lava that went down my gullet to see which would reach my stomach first and putrefy my supper.

"Gaaaghhhh!!!" My eyes watered up, and then the whiskey conspired with the truck heater to send signals to my brain that it was time to sweat—moisture rolled from my forehead and armpits—I yanked off my jacket.

Carl looked at me and grinned. "Good stuff, ain't it?"

"Damn right!" I croaked.

I had recovered sufficiently by the time we circled the block. Carl stopped the truck just ahead of the walking girls, and I rolled down the window.

"Hi... you girls wanna ride?"

One of them pulled away the muffler from her face. It was Elizabeth Hukala who was eleven years old. The street light reflected off of her braces as she gave me a wicked snarl.

"You guys better quit bothering us, or I'll get my brother Mutt to beat the pee outta you!"

Our tires spun snow as we pulled away. "Boy! From now on we don't stop fer any girls we haven't identified first! Jeez! Eleven years old!"

"Sounds like a damn good idea, Carl."

We cruised up by the Lutheran church which frequently held youth activities on Saturday nights. Now, the Lutheran church may not be the best place in the world to go looking for loose women, but time was marching on, and we had to cover all possibilities.

Carl reached in his hip pocket, pulled out his wallet, and dug out a small, round object.

"I dunno 'bout you, but I'm prepared just in case we come across a coupla hot ones." He handed me a foil-wrapped prophylactic.

"Carl, how long you had this in yer wallet?"

"Ah...I dunno... a while, I guess. Why?"

"Cause, the wallet's worn the foil away, an' I think there's a hole in the rubber." I handed it back to him.

Carl stopped the truck under a street light by the church and inspected the packet. "Yeah...I guess yer right...one'a these days I'll hafta get a new one."

"An, just outta curiosity, if that's whatcha got in mind, there'd be four of us in the cab of this pickup truck. How would you..."

Carl gave me a thoughtful stare. "Yeah, that'll be tricky all right...but I'll think a sumthin."

We were just about ready to move on when the church door opened, and two girls came out. Carl pointed excitedly.

"Hey! That's Beverly Salo and Adele Hendrickson from our class! Let's pick 'em up—I'll take Adele, an' you take Beverly."

"Can't do it."

"Whaddaya mean ya can't do it? Why not?"

"Cause Beverly's my cousin."

"Come on...how can she be yer cousin? You're not related to any a the Salos."

"Well...her mother's brother, Rieno Setala, is married to the sister of my uncle's second wife."

"That don't make her your cousin, does it?"

"She thinks it does. Who d'ya think told me?"

"Well, OK then. I'll take Beverly, an' you take Adele."

"No...Adele's my cousin too. Ya see, her uncle Matt..."

Carl slapped the steering wheel. "Ferget it! Ferget it! We should'a went by the Catholic church instead. Or, are ya related to all the Catholics too?"

"Maybe we outta go down to Marquette."

Carl looked at the gas gauge. "I got less than a quarter tank a gas an' about a buck to get through the night. How about you—how much you got?"

"About a buck an' a quarter."

"Well, that pretty much decides that we stay in town tonight."

"Let's go check the Bumblebee an' see who's around there."

The Bumblebee Cafe was one of the few eateries in town, and the food wasn't anything to write home about, but it was the only place within twenty miles where you could get French fries, so it usually pulled in a lot of the high school kids on weekends.

We were about a block away from the Bumblebee when we spotted another pair of girls heading toward the cafe.

Carl slowed down the truck behind them and put his nose close to the windshield in studied concentration. "That's Alice Maki an' Faye LaCroix—you aren't related to either one a them are'ya?"

"Not as far as I know."

"So, whattaya think?"

"I dunno, that Alice Maki has a pretty sharp tongue..."

"Yeah, but she's also gotta pretty sharp body too, in case you haven't noticed."

"Yeah...that's true..."

"Well then, let's go an' park by the Bumblebee, an' when they get there we'll jus' get outta the truck an' start talkin' to 'em like it wuz a coincidental meetin' or sumthin'."

"I gotta better idea. Go up to Chub Mattila's Standard station."

"What for?"

"'Cause if we go into the Bumblebee with them, we're gonna get stuck with the whole bill for whatever they order. We'll kill 'bout ten minutes at Chub's, give the girls a chance to order, an' then come in an' sit with them."

Carl gave me an admiring look. "That's usin' the old noodle!"

We drove over to the Standard station where we wisely invested in a couple of bottles of 7-Up in case the girls didn't go for straight whiskey and wanted mixed drinks instead. When we thought the time was right we drove over to the Bumblebee Cafe.

Our timing couldn't have been better. Alice and Faye had just been served cheeseburgers, Coca-Cola, and French fries and were handing money over to Thelma Olson, the Bumblebee waitress. We put on our most charming smiles and sat down with them in the booth.

Alice dipped a fry in a puddle of catsup on her plate and eyed me suspiciously. It wasn't too many years ago that Alice had been one of the boys, killing rats with a slingshot at the town dump, and helping the Finn kids chuck iron ore at the French and Italian kids. When things got dull, we even used to throw iron ore at each other. Now that we were in our mid teens, the game had changed, but neither of us had any experience with the new ground rules.

I casually reached for a French fry on Alice's plate. "So...how are you girls tonight?"

With the speed of a striking cobra, Alice lashed out with her right and knocked the fry out of my hand. "If you want French fries, Thelma'll be happy to take your order!"

As a matter of fact, Thelma had been watching my abortive courtship maneuver and sidled up behind me.

"You guys wanna order anything or are'ya jus' gonna sit there an' take abuse from these young ladies?" She snapped her chewing gum sarcastically.

I did a quick mental calculation to determine what I could afford. I could get a cheeseburger, fries, and a Nesbitt's Orange, but that would leave me with about sixty cents to last me through most of next week. I took the plunge, and Carl did the same.

Alice must have figured that she would have to quit slugging guys if her social life was going to improve, because she offered me a fry while we waited for our order. While we were making small talk, I was going over in my mind what subterfuge we would have to use to get the girls into the pickup truck. But, Carl took the initiative.

"Say...I hear that there's a passenger plane taking off from the Marquette Airport for Green Bay at ten o'clock tonight. We were thinking about drivin' down there to watch it. You girls wanna come along?"

I couldn't believe he had said that! We didn't have much gas in the truck and between the two of us we were probably going to have less than a dollar after we paid for our food. I looked at him questioningly, but he just sat there with an oily grin on his face.

The girls looked at each other with shy smiles. I could see that Carl had struck a chord with the airplane idea. I whipped out a pencil and started to work out the mathematics on a paper napkin. Round trip mileage to the Marquette Airport...probable miles per gallon of the truck...price for a gallon of regular at Chub's Standard station...present net worth of Carl and myself...yep, it was going to be close, but we just might make it. I'd have to remember to drain the gas-pump hose into the truck when we stopped the pump.

Faye let out a little giggle. "Well, we really shouldn't do it, but it does sound like fun. What do you think, Alice?"

"It's OK with me." Alice looked over at me. "What were you doing on that napkin?"

"Oh...it's just an algebra problem from my homework that I had been thinking about." I leered inwardly. This was going to be a great night! Cuddled up at the end of the runway...protecting Alice's ears as the plane roared over our heads... maybe we could even tell them that there was another plane coming in from Detroit at midnight. This had endless possibilities.

Thelma brought our food and laid it out in front of Carl and me as Faye and Alice were finishing up their cheeseburgers. I was fishing out my money when Thelma glanced at the girls.

"Kin I get you girls anything else?"

Faye said, "You know? I'm still a little bit hungry, and it's a long way to Marquette. I think I'll have one of your pieces of rhubarb pie...and put a scoop of vanilla ice cream on it too."

Alice said, "Yeah...make that two!"

Thelma turned to me with a villainous sneer. "Shall I jus' put that on the bill of the big spenders here?"

I nodded dumbly as I crumpled up the napkin filled with calculations. My night of romance and passion had just been torpedoed by rhubarb pie a la mode. That was going to cost us an extra sixty cents, and there was no way in hell we were going to get to the airport with what little money we had left. I don't think Carl had any idea of the true extent of our dilemma, since he was still grinning broadly as he bit into his cheeseburger.

We finished up the food and were getting up to leave when Alice leaned over and whispered to me.

"I think we ought'a leave Thelma a tip since she's such a good waitress...don't you think so?"

"Yeah, terrific waitress." I slipped a nickel under my plate.

As we were going out, I pulled Carl aside. "How're we gonna get to the airport? We're almost broke, and no gas!"

"Who's goin' to the airport?"

"But, the airplane at ten o'clock..."

"You think I'm an expert on airplane schedules?"

"But, you tol' them...what're we gonna do?"

He just grinned. "Leave it to me."

Alice's face dropped when she saw the pickup truck. "A truck? Where're we all gonna sit?"

I didn't have the foggiest idea what Carl had in mind, but I had a brilliant idea about the seating arrangements.

"Carl'll be driving, Faye sits in the middle, an' you sit on my lap."

"You want me to sit on your lap all the way to Marquette?"

"Sure. It'll work out fine."

"You better not try any funny stuff, mister!"

We all piled into the cab of the truck. The girls both had on full-length woolen coats and Carl and I were dressed in our usual mackinaws. It was like cramming four bears into a clothes closet. Delicately, Alice lowered herself onto my lap. My knees creaked in protest. Gawd! I didn't realize that girls were so heavy! Probably all that rhubarb pie a la mode coming home to roost.

Carl started up the engine, gunned it a few times and turned a critical ear to the dashboard.

"Y'hear that funny sound, Jer? Yup! It's jus' like I told Chub the other day. This thing's gettin' ready to throw a rod. I wouldn't give 'er another thirty miles before it happens."

Actually, old man Kettu's pickup truck had so many funny sounds that it was capable of throwing almost anything at any given time, but I nodded my head knowingly.

"Yeah, it sounds bad all right."

Faye looked alarmed. "What does that mean?"

Carl gave her a crestfallen look. "Well, I'm afraid we'd better not try to make it to the Marquette Airport tonight. I'd hate to be stuck out there on US-41 in this cold weather. I got more consideration for you girls than that."

Alice reached for the door handle. "Well, I guess we'd better get out and..."

Carl hastily interrupted. "But, there's no reason why we can't drive around town tonight. I can tell by the sound that we'll be OK for awhile."

Alice sniffed skeptically. "Why am I thinking that this is some kind of flim-flam job?"

Carl put the truck in gear and reached over and put the heater on full blast. The snow squeaked under the tires as we pulled away from the Bumblebee Cafe in search of romantic adventure.

Within two blocks, the climate in the cab became a reasonable facsimile of a Finnish sauna. All of the windows fogged up with condensation, and beads of sweat started to roll down my chest and collect in my navel.

Carl stopped the truck and took off his mackinaw. "It's finally starting to get comfortable in here," he said, as he pulled his ski sweater off over his head. "Anybody else wanna take anything off?"

The girls just sat there, perfectly comfortable in their coats, mufflers, mittens, and knitted kerchiefs. Alice finally said to Faye, "When he gets down to the long underwear, I'm walking home." I was helpless to take anything off, being in a state of semi-paralysis with Alice on top of me.

We got underway again and proceeded down Fire Street. As was frequently the case, the township hadn't gotten around to putting gravel on the hill by the firehouse and the icy hard-packed snow made it treacherously slippery. Carl got to the top of the hill above the firehouse and turned to me with a quick wink.

"It looks pretty slippery here, huh, Jer? If yer not careful you can get into a..." He paused for dramatic effect. "A spin-out!"

This was a signal between Carl and me that one of his favorite sports was about to begin. Carl had been practicing spin-outs ever since the snow had covered the roads that winter. A spin-out wasn't that hard to get into—you went down the road at fairly high speed, slammed on the brakes, and pulled the steering wheel violently to the left. The vehicle would go into a flat counterclockwise spin, still moving in the direction you were originally headed, but rotating at the same time. The true artistry of spin-outs was in getting the vehicle to rotate far enough so that the front end came around full circle, pointing in its original direction, then down-shifting and giving it gas at the right time, to pull out of the spin and continue on your way. But, you had to pick your time and place with care. The roadway had to be slick, hard-packed snow with no traffic, parked cars, or people. Like drag racing of the next decade, it was a sport of teen-age boys, to be practiced covertly.

Carl had it firmly planted in his mind that fright and passion were emotions that went hand in hand. Last summer he had been to the Marquette County Fair with Lucille Erikson. They had gone on the Caterpillar, a ride of modest intensity where you went around an undulating track in a covered shell. Lucille had started to scream when the shell came over the seats, and she threw her arms around Carl's neck and hung on for the duration of the ride. Carl enjoyed it so much that he vowed that, at the earliest opportunity, he was going to scare the living daylights out of any girl sitting next to him. As he gunned the engine at the top of Fire Street hill, it was obvious that tonight was the earliest opportunity.

Carl wiped the fog from the driver's side of the windshield and launched the pickup truck down the hill. By the time we neared the firehouse at the bottom of the hill, we were doing about forty. Carl started to insert dramatic dialog into the maneuver.

"Uh-oh...I think I'm losing control...I'm...going into a SPIN-OUT!!!" And with that, he slammed on the brakes and whipped the steering wheel hard to the left.

I had been in spin-outs with Carl before, so I was prepared for what the truck was going to do. What I wasn't prepared for, was what the girls were going to do. As we went into the spin, Faye started to flail her arms around wildly, and I caught a vicious elbow right in the nose. Alice started to lose her balance on my lap, and reaching out for something to hang on to, grabbed my right ear, and almost tore it off my head. Why was I being punished? This was all Carl's idea!

The truck slid by the firehouse sideways, spinning counterclockwise as it went down the street. In the cab it was like looking in a kaleidoscope filled with fuzzy snowbanks, wool coats, mittens, and open mouths. The truck swung around full circle, and Carl jammed it into second gear and floored the gas petal. The back wheels dug in, and we pulled out of the spin and continued down Fire Street as though nothing had happened. Carl, grinning, pulled the truck over to the side of the road and stopped, no doubt waiting for Faye to throw her arms around his neck in gratitude for pulling us out of a dangerous situation.

Faye threw up in his lap.

"Oh...oh...oh, my! I'm sorry! It's just that I always get queasy riding in a car...oh...oh, my!" She wiped her face with her wool scarf.

Alice spoke through clenched teeth. "What're you sorry for? This idiot brought it on himself! C'mon Faye, let's walk home! You'll feel better in the fresh air."

But, Faye was still apologizing. "No, no, I don't want to be a wet blanket on the evening. Let me get out and eat some snow and I'll be OK."

We all got out of the truck and tended to ourselves. Carl had some rags underneath the seat, and he did the best he could with these to clean off his pants. My nose was bleeding, and my right ear was starting to swell up. I mopped up the blood as best I could with my bandanna. Faye ate several handfuls of snow, and washed her face with it. Alice just stood there, quietly steaming.

Carl then hatched his next brilliant idea. He pulled out the Castoria bottle out of his pocket and offered it to Alice.

"You think that I need a laxative after that ride? You gotta be the weirdest guy I know!"

"It's jus' a lil' whiskey...I thought it might settle you down a lil' bit." Carl unscrewed the cap and started to put it up to his mouth.

"Put that away! If that's the way you drive when you're sober, I sure don't want to see your driving when you've got half a snootful!"

Faye interrupted. "Look, let's not fight...I really feel much better now. Let's get back into the truck. We can still drive around a little bit."

So our evening of heavenly romance got back on the rails. The cab of the truck now had a new gamy pungency to add to the bouquet of moist bodies and wet wool.

Once again, Carl became his old unflappable self, and as we drove through Frenchtown, he pulled out his Bull Durham and Zig-Zag papers. Oh, no, I thought, he was going to show us his flaming cigarette trick!

The girls watched in fascination as Carl built the cigarette while we slowly cruised along the snowy streets. As usual, the final product had the shape of a python that had swallowed a large pig. Carl pulled out a kitchen match and struck it with his thumbnail. It didn't light. Carl scowled and dug his thumbnail deep into the head of the match and gave it a mighty scratch. The match head snapped off and wedged underneath his thumbnail. We all looked at it for a second before it burst into flame.

"OW!!!...OW!!!...OW!!!...OW!!!" Carl shook his flaming thumb through the air trying to put out the fire. It went out in a second, but it must have seemed like a lifetime to him. He stared in horror at the blackened spot on his thumb.

"Ice! I need some ice! They say yer supposed to put ice on a burn! I'm goin' over to the IGA store an' buy some ice!"

Alice spoke up. "You wanna buy some ice? We're here in Marquette County of the U.P., in the dead of winter, under five feet of snow, an' you wanna *BUY* some ice? I don't think you're smart enough to make it through high school! Go an' make a snowball an' stick your thumb in it."

If that's the way you drive sober...

"Yeah. That's what I'll do...make a snowball."

Carl got out and made his snowball and came around to the passenger side with his thumb stuck in it. "Jer, I think yer gonna hafta drive."

Alice had an opinion about that too. "Oh, great! Now we're getting a driver who's still three months short of qualifying for a driver's license!"

That was one thing I always hated about living in a small town. Everybody had the complete book on your religion, personal habits, and vital statistics. We untangled ourselves, and I got behind the wheel. Somehow, it had become an unspoken agreement that Alice was my date and Faye was Carl's, so now Alice sat in the middle and Faye sat on Carl's lap. After grinding the gears, we got underway. I decided to give the evening one more fling and made a turn onto the river road going out of town.

Alice looked at me. "Now, where are you going? Aren't you gonna take us home? Haven't you had enough?"

"Oh...I dunno, I jus' thought we'd ride out along the river for awhile. The moon might look kinda pretty, shining off the ice on the river."

"That really sounds romantic all right," she said sarcastically, "And, I suppose you thought that we might do a little necking...you with blood dripping out of your nose, and your friend sitting there with his thumb stuck in a snowball."

I was making a mental note to cross Alice off my list of datable women as we approached a sweeping curve on the river road. I pushed the clutch in to shift from second to third, but I evidently didn't have it in far enough, because the transmission growled and the floor-mounted gear shift lever bucked in my hand. My hand popped off the gear shift knob and shot between Alice's legs.

What happened then is still a little hazy in my mind. I remember that Alice hauled off and belted me in the right ear...the same one that she had tried to rip off twenty minutes earlier. A bolt of intense pain shot through my head, and I took my hands off the wheel. The next time I looked out the windshield the truck was headed for the shoulder of the road which sloped down to the river. I jammed on the brakes, but the pickup slid off the road, plowed through several small poplar trees and banged into a couple of birch trees above the river's edge. The truck was tilted over about forty-five degrees with the passenger door resting firmly against the biggest birch tree.

We all sat there in shock for several seconds. We were an Alice-and-Faye sandwich, with Carl as the bottom crust, wedged up against the passenger door, and me on top. I pushed up, trying to open the driver's door but it wouldn't budge. Gasoline fumes started to drift into the cab.

Carl looked up at me calmly and said, "I think we better get outta here before she catches on fire."

That was all that the girls needed to hear. They both grabbed me and rammed me up into the driver's door, which popped open. Faye got a better footing by planting one of her galoshes on the side of Carl's face, and together they lifted me and threw me up and out of the door into the snow.

I lay there staring at the rusting underside of the truck when Alice jumped out of the truck, one foot landing on my rib cage. I rolled out of the way just in time to avoid Faye when she landed. The girls scrambled up through the snow to the road and stood there glaring at us.

Carl and I got up to the road, and the four of us just stood there looking at the disaster. What had happened had just started to dawn on me. Carl's old man was going to kill me if I didn't die from the injuries I sustained during the evening.

Headlights appeared, and a flat-bed logging truck, with chains on the dual rear wheels, stopped. Arne Mattson got out. Arne was nineteen years old, about six foot three, blonde, Nordic, and handsome—I hated guys who looked like that.

"Looks like you need some help here."

We nodded silently.

Arne looked at the pickup truck and went to his cab and got out a tow chain. "I think I can get your truck back on the road with this." He wrapped the chain around the rear axle of the pickup and attached the other end to his truck. With no difficulty, he pulled the pickup back on to the road. Carl got behind the wheel, and the truck started right up. The only apparent damage was a large dent in the right front fender.

Alice gave Arne a sweet smile. "Arne, would you give Faye and me a ride back to town? It's getting late, and we have to get home."

"Sure..." he looked at Carl and me. "Are you guys goin' to be all right? Ya know, you shouldn't be drivin' on this road without chains."

Alice looked at us and sniffed. "Oh...they have chains all right...around their brains!"

My nose had started to bleed again, and I dabbed at it with my bandanna as I watched Carl work over the dented fender with a ball-peen hammer. We had driven the pickup over to the Standard station, taken off the right front wheel, and Carl was in the midst of trying to straighten out the dent made by the birch tree. What he had succeeded in doing with the hammer was to transform the one large dent into many small dents. The truck now looked like it had goose bumps from the cold.

Chub Mattila finished up a lube job and came over to the truck, wiping his hands on a greasy rag.

"What happened to you guys? You look awful!"

Gingerly, I poked my aching ribs to see if I could feel any broken bones. "We were out on a double date."

"An' they did that to you?" He looked closely at Carl. "Carl, d'ya know you gotta a footprint on the left side of your face? What kind'a women d'you guys go out with anyhow?"

American Graffiti was drawing to a close. Harrison Ford had just blown the big drag race when he lost control of his Chevy and piled it up in the boondocks. The brunette had run back to Ronny Howard with open arms and Harrison just stood there, clutching an injured arm, his ego badly bruised.

I grunted with satisfaction as I went to the refrigerator for another Diet Cherry Coke. You just got a taste of how the real world turns, Harrison! How do you like it?

The Last Run of the
Black Widow-Maker

Seventy-five, eighty, eighty-five, eighty-six, eighty-seven, eighty-eight, eighty-nine...and ninety." My last dollar landed on top of the stack of bills on the kitchen table in front of Arne Setala, an old Finn dairy farmer who lived outside of town.

I could have told you where every single dollar in that pile came from: potato picking, cash presents from birthdays and Christmases, and soda jerking at a local restaurant for the princely sum of five dollars a week.

Arne took a large leather coin purse out of a breast pocket in his bib overalls and put the cash away. He fished a crumpled piece of paper out of another pocket, wet the point of a pencil on his tongue, and signed the paper.

"This here's the owner's certificate. You send it in to Lansing an' you'll get one with yer name on it inna coupla weeks."

I took the paper and stared at it, but the only thing that registered was that I'd just bought my first car. I looked out the window at it sitting on the grass by the kitchen door. A black, two-door, 1930 Model A Ford. A little shopworn to be sure, but it had all its vital organs, and it was all mine, free and clear.

The Model A Ford wasn't built for speed. It had a tall boxlike chassis with a vertical windshield, and it was powered by a spunky little four-cylinder engine which, when idling, sounded like a dog on a hot day. But the price was right, and my old man had looked at it and had given his approval.

Arne put the ignition key on the table. "You'll have'ta git a new battery one a these days. The one that's in there don't hold a charge worth a damn. An' the right rear tire keeps leaking air. The tube needs a patch somewhere."

Nobody could ever accuse Arne of giving them the hard sell.

I snatched the key from the table and tore out to the car. MINE! ALL MINE!...I jumped behind the wheel, started it up, and backed out of the yard.

The old man stuck his head out of the kitchen door and yelled, "Ain't you gonna give Arne a ride home?"

I sped off.

For the next several hours I reached heights of ecstasy I never dreamed possible. Like a man and woman in a sexual embrace, the Model A and I cruised the township roads with abandon, laughing recklessly as we spewed gravel on the hairpin turns. In my haste, I fumbled in my attempts to consummate the union as quickly as possible—several times killing the engine by popping the clutch prematurely. But like an experienced and forgiving seductress, she started right up again and purred contentedly as we piled up mile after mile. We finally got back home as dusk was settling in. I got out in a state of happy fulfillment. I patted her warm metallic breast and went in for supper.

The next morning the honeymoon was over.

Before breakfast, I ran out to warm up the engine so I could drive to school and show her off. I punched the starter, but like an aging floozy who had one too many the night before, she went "Uuuggghhh..." and lapsed into silence. The battery was dead.

I was laboriously trying to arouse her interest by hand-cranking the engine, when I heard footsteps behind me.

"You bought Arne Setala's Model A?" My pal, Lee Campbell, was appraising the car skeptically.

"Yep. Gave him the money yesterday."

"But, I thought you were hot for Frank Nardi's '33 Chevy coupe."

"Well, he wants a hundred an' fifty bucks for it an' I didn't have it."

"But, I thought he said you could pay him the rest later."

I straightened up from the cranking job and wiped my forehead with a bandanna. "Look, don't blab this around, but the old man wouldn't let me buy it 'cause he said it was too fast a car."

"Too fast? How does he know? He doesn't even drive!"

"He listened to the engine and said it was too fast a car."

"So, he must have liked the 'bucketa-bucketa' sound of this four cylinder."

"I guess so. Anyway, this is what I got. It was goin' good yesterday, but the battery's deader'n hell this morning."

Lee was sitting behind the wheel. "Jeez, I never seen so much play in a steering wheel before. You can swing it a full quarter turn without it turning the front wheels. Must be a bitch to steer."

"Yeah, it takes some gettin' used to. I'm goin' to put a necker's knob on the steering wheel. That'll make it a little easier."

A necker's knob was a plastic doorknob-shaped attachment that clamped on the outer rim of a steering wheel to allow the driver to make one-handed maneuvers. It had become a sexual status symbol among male teenage drivers, being a mute statement that it was necessary to steer the car with the left hand because the right hand was busily engaged with a female passenger. In my case, it was to become a matter of pure survival.

Lee got out of the car. "Whew! You oughta get some of your mother's perfume for this thing! I think Arne was hauling some of his cows in the back seat. You know that your right rear tire is low?"

"Look, I know it's gotta few things that need fixing. As soon as I get it started, I'm gonna get Chub Mattila up at the Standard station to look the whole thing over for me."

Lee grinned. "Well, your old man oughta be happy with you driving this car. It sure ain't no widow-maker."

I paused with my cranking. "Widow-Maker. That's what I'll call it!"

Lee looked at the black paint. "How about the Black Widow-Maker? That really sounds dangerous! Hahahahahaha."

Chub Mattila wiped his hands on a greasy rag and fished a Lucky Strike out of his breast pocket.

"Well, that battery is just about shot. That's what I been tellin' Arne Setala every time he brought 'er in for a quick charge."

I disconnected the air hose from the valve on the right rear tire. "Quick charge?"

"Yeah. You put the battery on the charger an' turn the juice up high for an hour or so. It's cheap, but after awhile it fries your battery."

"How much is a quick charge?"

"Two bits."

"An' how much is a regular charge?"

"A buck."

"Gimme a quick charge."

"OK. The battery wouldn't run down so fast if you put new brushes in the generator."

"Brushes?"

He opened up the hood on the Model A and pointed. "That's the generator."

"OK."

He unscrewed a cover plate on the generator. "An' these black things are the brushes. They don't cost much an' you can put 'em in yourself."

I grabbed the steering wheel and whipped it back and forth. "How about this play in the steering wheel?"

Chub lit up his Lucky Strike. "The worm gear in the steering box is shot. I can put a new one in, but it'll cost ya."

"I'm gonna put a necker's knob on the wheel an' try to get by with that."

He grabbed the wheel and whipped it a full ninety degrees or more. "That'll make for exciting drivin'". He went around to the open hood and pulled out the oil dipstick. "Ya know? Arne had this car for about eight or nine years an' never changed the oil." He put the dripping black stick under my nose.

"Does it need changing?"

He took a drag from his cigarette. "You don't know much about cars, do ya?"

"Uhhh...nope. I guess not."

"Well, you'll get plenty a chances to learn with this heap...I tell ya what. Old man Saari brings in his Buick for lube and oil change every two thousand miles. The next time he comes in, I'll give you his old oil for nothin'. It'll be better than that sludge you got in there now."

I broke into a grin for the first time that day. "Hey, that's great!"

Chub hooked the charger to the battery. "I thought you were gonna buy Nardi's '33 Chevy coupe. Now, that's a nice car!"

"Awww...go to he... Well...thanks a lot, Chub. I'll pick up the car in about an hour."

For the next several weeks I became immersed in a do-it-yourself course in auto repair. Generator brushes were replaced. Tubes were extracted from tires and tested for leaks in my mother's washtub. My bedroom reeked from the vulcanizing agent on tube patches. My old man lost a bet with our neighbor when he wagered that the Widow-Maker would never run again after I completely disassembled the carburetor, cleaned it, and put it back in the car. The final touch was loading up a bug-spray gun with Aqua Velva and fumigating the inside. The Black Widow-Maker was ready for her social debut.

The Last Run of the Black Widow-Maker

Alice Maki gathered up her skirt and crinoline petticoats and carefully threaded her way between the mud puddles from her kitchen door to the Widow-Maker. Tonight she was a vision of exquisite beauty. It seemed like only last year that we were standing shoulder to shoulder, slinging chunks of iron ore to ward off the advances of the French and Italian kids during the pitched battles of the notorious Frenchtown Wars.

She eyed the Widow-Maker dubiously as I opened the passenger door.

"So...you bought Arne Setala's car...well...it looks like a nice one."

"Thanks. It needed some work, but I got 'er runnin' pretty good now." In fact, I had blown a dollar today and gotten the expensive trickle charge for the battery to insure that I wouldn't have to get all sweaty cranking the engine tonight.

It was the first Friday in April, and tonight was the pinnacle of the high school's social calendar—the Junior Prom. The floor of the basketball court in the school gymnasium had been waxed to a high gloss for the evening's festivities. The services of a Wurlitzer juke box had been graciously donated for the occasion. It promised to be a gala affair.

Alice looked around the inside of the car as we started up. "I've never ridden in one of these before. It's interesting. The inside kind'a smells like shaving lotion."

She looked at me with alarm as we sped down the gravel road. "What's wrong with the steering wheel? Is it coming off?"

"Naw! It's OK. The steering gear's a little worn is all. It works fine once you get used to it."

I had bought a necker's knob in Marquette the week before. It was a thing of beauty with a picture of a Lockheed Lightning P-38 encased in clear plastic. I had, in fact, gotten used to steering the Widow-Maker, but with ninety degrees of play in the wheel, it looked like I was furiously scrubbing the inside of the windshield with an invisible rag as I drove. To illustrate that I had total control, I shifted the necker's knob from my right hand to my left and put my right arm on the top of her seat.

Alice gave me a frosty stare. "If you think that you're gonna steer a car with steering that bad with one hand while you make grabs at me with the other, you got another think comin'. Both hands on the wheel!"

We bucketa-bucketa'd along in the gathering twilight. I turned my head and looked her over.

"You look really nice tonight."

She gave me a thin smile. "Thanks, but I really hate to have to sit there for two hours while my mother curls my hair. It's a lot of work to get ready for one of these. At least we won't get rained on like last year."

Last year's Junior Prom ended up in a total disaster. I didn't have a car at my disposal, and while we were walking home, a thunderstorm came up and drenched us.

"Yeah. The Widow-Maker'll keep us dry."

"Is that what you call the car?"

"Yup."

"Why do you call it that?"

"It's sort of a joke. A widow-maker is something fast and dangerous. This car ain't exactly that."

The signs of spring were everywhere. The dwindling snowbanks had turned an ugly shade of gray-black, and the gravel roads were pockmarked with numerous mud puddles.

But for sheer splendor of size and depth, no mud puddle ever matched the Swedetown Puddle.

Swedetown was on top of a large hill, and every spring the runoff from the melting snow created a monster puddle at the base of the Swedetown hill. The puddle was about one hundred yards long, at least a foot deep in the middle, and stretched across the whole road. It had become an annual challenge to local drivers to test the robustness of their ignition system by roaring through the Swedetown Puddle at top speed without killing the engine.

In the Upper Peninsula, people took amusement wherever they found it.

The Swedetown Puddle loomed ahead in all its quiet majesty, and I pressed down on the gas pedal. The engine went from its sedate bucketa-bucketa to bucka-bucka-bucka-bucka.

Alice pursed her lips and looked at me. "You're not gonna play that silly game with this puddle, are you?"

"The Widow-Maker'll make it through jus' fine!"

BUCKA-BUCKA-BUCKA-
SSSPPPPLLLLLUUUSSSHHHHHHIIIISSSSSSSSSS!!!

We had hit the puddle at forty miles an hour: the water had pounded up against the hot muffler and turned to steam. Unfortunately, the wooden floorboards had several cracks, and the steam, accompanied by atomized mud, exploded into the car. We had an instant sauna, and the visibility went to zero. I quickly turned on the windshield wiper, but the condensation was on the inside!

If the Swedetown Puddle had killed the engine, the damage would have been lessened, but the Widow-Maker roared right on through as if nothing was happening, and in all the excitement I didn't have enough sense to slow down.

Alice's only comment on the proceedings was:

"AAAUUUUGGGGGGHHHHH!!!!!!!"

On the other side of the puddle, I pulled the car to the side of the road to access the damage. The legs of my suit pants were soaking wet, and my shoes had lost the brilliant gloss that I had painstakingly put on them an hour ago, but it was nothing that couldn't be fixed.

Alice, however, was a different story.

The fluffy petticoats under her dress had deflated like a leaky balloon, and her dress had acquired a liberal lacing of brown polka dots. Her exquisitely curled blonde hair was unwinding before my eyes. But, what really sent chills down my spine was that the steam had completely fogged up her glasses and made her appear as if she had huge, circular white eyes, with no pupils. I was looking at a homicidal Little Orphan Annie.

"Taaake meeee hoooome...," she hissed.

Elaine Olsen leaned forward from the rear seat of the Widow-Maker and folded her arms across the top of the front passenger seat.

"Is Alice really going to go with us? I never saw her so mad as when I talked to her the Monday after the prom. I didn't think she even knew words like that!"

Lee Campbell, Elaine, and I were driving over to Alice's house two weeks after the prom. The occasion was the grand opening of the Evergreen Drive-In Theater on US-41. We had never had a drive-in theater in Marquette County before, and everyone who had a car or truck was definitely going to be there.

I turned my head slightly from the artful task of steering the Widow-Maker. "Oh, yeah. She's OK now. I told her that I've fixed the floorboards. An' besides, she really wants to see the drive-in."

I didn't know what movie was being shown at the Evergreen that night, but it mattered little. The word had quickly spread around the male teen-age ranks that drive-in movies were ideal places to make out. I had casually asked Lee if he wanted to drive the Widow-Maker, picturing Alice and me snuggled up in the back seat, but he declined, stating that he didn't think he was up to the steering.

Alice opened the car door and carefully inspected the floor. I had bought some rubber stair tread covers and nailed them to the wooden floorboards.

"Don't worry. She's watertight now," I assured her.

She pushed her glasses up the bridge of her nose and sniffed. "I hope your mother doesn't break her neck on the stairs that you took these from."

We had pulled onto US-41, and the Widow-Maker was purring contently. The weather was balmy and clear, and my razor-like repartee, enhancing the conversation, had even brought a smile or two to Alice's face.

CLUNK!!!CLUNK!!!!!SSSCCCRRREEEEEEEEEEEEEEEEE!!!!!!

The steering wheel snapped viciously to the right. Hanging onto it for dear life, I slammed on the brakes. The Widow-Maker went into a flat skid and came to rest on the shoulder.

Alice dug her fingernails deep into my right biceps.

"WWHHHAAAAAATTTTTT!!!!!
WHATSSITT DOING NOWWWW?????"

I disengaged her fingers from my arm. "I dunno." Turning off the ignition, I scrambled out and ran to the front of the car.

The problem didn't require any deep analysis. The right side of the front bumper had come loose from its bracket, fallen to the highway, and wedged underneath the right front wheel. Needless to say, the bolt that held it onto the bracket was nowhere to be seen.

I walked over to Alice's window. "It's OK. It's just the bumper came loose."

But, Alice wasn't about to be pacified.

"THIS CAR IS OUT TO GET ME!!!
IT DIDN'T DO A COMPLETE JOB ON THE NIGHT
OF THE PROM, AND NOW IT'S TRYING AGAIN!!!"

"Don' be silly, Alice. We'll get 'er fixed in a jiffy."

Lee got out of the car and inspected the damage. "We better go back up the road an' see if we can find that bolt."

But dusk was settling in rapidly, and the bolt was nowhere to be seen. Lee and I were walking back to the car when I was hit with a sudden inspiration.

"Hey! My fishing rod is in the back of the car! We'll tie up the bumper with fish line!"

We went about our task with dispatch, pulling several yards of fish line from the reel and tying the right-hand end of the bumper to the bolt hole in the right bracket. I started her up and we bucketa-bucketa'd off to the Evergreen Drive-In. Alice was still babbling to no one in particular.

The Last Run of the Black Widow-Maker

The drive-in movie was a wondrous adventure, with the main feature being a technicolor western of fairly recent vintage, starring Randolph Scott. But, Alice was in no mood for light romance, or even polite conversation for that matter. My attempt to put her in a better frame of mind with an extra-large tub of buttered popcorn and a Nesbitt's Orange drink fell short of the mark.

The movie ended, and the drive-in erupted with starting engines and headlights. I gloomily started up the Widow-Maker, realizing that yet another date with Alice was approaching a tragic conclusion. We were waiting patiently in the line of cars queued at the exit when I realized that the guy in front of me had stalled his car. It was a brand-new, dark blue 1950 Packard.

My head snapped up with another inspiration! Giving this expensive new car a push would redeem the Widow-Maker!

"This guy looks like he needs some help. I'll ask him if he wants a push." I started to get out.

Alice grabbed my arm, which still throbbed from her fingernails. "Wait a minute. You mean to tell me that you want to push that car with...with this? Look at it! It's brand new! It musta cost thousands of dollars! What if you did something to it?"

"It's just a push! What could go wrong? At least mine's running!"

Casually I strolled up to the Packard's window. The driver was a big beefy guy, who was with his wife and two little kids. "You want a push?"

He was busy grinding the starter, but finally looked up. "Yeah, I guess so. I think I flooded 'er. It's got some new kind'a choke that I'm not used to. I've only had 'er a week."

"Don't worry. The exit road's clear now, an' I'll get you goin'."

I pulled up the Widow-Maker and touched bumpers. He put the Packard in neutral, and we started to move up the exit road to US-41. When we got going about twenty five miles an hour, he popped his clutch.

That's when things started to happen very fast.

The resistance of the Packard being in gear pushed the Widow-Maker's front bumper over his back bumper, and we momentarily locked up. I had put on my brakes to give him room to get his engine started, but when I realized that the bumpers were locked, I swung the wheel to the left in an attempt to get them loose. The Packard's rear bumper then started to pull the right side of my bumper out from the front end of the Widow-Maker.

In that fraction of a second I remembered...gawd!!! My bumper is tied on with fish line!

To the credit of the manufacturer, that fish line far exceeded the poundage it was rated for, but when the right side of my bumper got about a foot and a half out from the bracket, it snapped, and the bumper broke loose from the Packard at the same time.

The Widow-Maker's bumper became one gigantic tuning fork. With a mighty:

WWWHHHHHHAAAANNNNGGGGG!!!!!!!!!

it sprang back, bounced off of its bracket, then forward again, neatly emasculating the Packard by snipping off the shiny chrome trunk handle.

The four of us in my car saw the whole thing in my headlights, but all the Packard driver knew was that he hadn't gotten his car started, and something bad had happened. He got out of his car and started walking toward us.

Lee leaned over to me and whispered, "He's still stalled. Let's get out of here."

That sounded like excellent advice, so I put it in reverse, dragging my bumper with me. Then I put it in first gear and started to pull around him. As we passed, he was just figuring out what had happened, and he gave me a look that would have made Edward G. Robinson flinch.

The right wheel kept wanting to run over the end of the bumper dragging on the ground, and only by swinging the steering wheel back and forth did I make any headway. So we slowly snaked out the exit road, away from the scene of the crime.

Lee looked out of the rear window. "Jeeez! The guy's chasing us on foot! Step on it!!"

Alice, who had remained transfixed throughout the incident, suddenly came to life. She leaned out the right window.

"SIMMER DOWN, MISTER! YOU GOT OFF EASY!
YOU HAVE NO IDEA OF WHAT THIS CAR
IS CAPABLE OF DOING TO YOU!"

I pulled her back into the car. "Alice...shuddup!"

We went about two hundred yards down US-41 before we dared to stop. Lee and I quickly made another fish line repair to the bumper, and we proceeded home in silence.

Pulling up at Alice's house, I started to get out of the car. She grabbed me by the right arm again.

"No! Don't see me to the door! I'm not going to kiss you goodnight or anything else that you might have in mind! I have to run inside and write a letter to the State Police and tell them to come and get this car, for the safety of everybody living in Marquette County!" With that, she slammed the car door and disappeared into the night.

I just sat there for several seconds with my head on the steering wheel. "Ya know? Sometimes I think Alice and I aren't cut out for each other."

"YOU HAVE NO IDEA OF WHAT THIS CAR IS CAPABLE OF DOING TO YOU..."

Smoky La Farge clutched the baseball and squinted in at Clyde Bertucci for a sign. He wound up and threw a curve which snapped neatly into the catcher's mitt. Clyde looked over at Mutt Hukala who was taking it all in. "I bet you would'a looked foolish tryin' to hit that one, Mutt!"

Mutt took a drag from his Camel and snorted. "Look at that raggedy-assed ball! Half the stitching is loose! If they let Bob Feller throw a baseball like that, he could make it circle the batter's head a couple a times 'fore it dropped in the mitt!"

It was the first Friday in May and a bunch of us were spending lunch hour at Chub Mattila's Standard station, swapping lies and generally hanging around until we had to go back to school. Chub was changing the oil on a '48 De Soto, and I was eyeing the drained oil to see if it was worth putting into the Widow-Maker. Old man Saari still hadn't brought his Buick in.

Summer was definitely on the way. The last dirty snowbank had submerged into a murky pool and the temperature was consistently getting into the forties and fifties during the day.

Smoky La Farge hummed an impressive fastball in to his battery-mate and grinned at Mutt. "Get me a good baseball, an' I'll still make you Finns look like you jus' came over from the old country! Remember las' year's Fourth a July game? I seem t'remember that I struck out eleven a you."

Mutt exhaled his last drag and ground out the butt in the dirt. "Look, anytime you spaghetti snappers kin get nine a you together, I'll round up some guys and a few girls, an' we'll kick yer asses from here t'Marquette."

This friendly banter hailed the beginning of the township's baseball season. The schedule was flexible, with a game taking place any time we could get eighteen guys to the ball diamond. The league consisted of two teams: the Catholics and the Finns. Methodists were considered free agents, being drafted by either side as the need arose.

Smoky looked around the Standard station. He nodded his head at Punk Valentti who was checking over Chub's used-tire supply. "Punk, why don' you run down t'yer street an' pick up Arquette and Tony. I think we kin 'commodate these clowns right now! How 'bout it, Mutt? Ya wanna cut school this afternoon an' go out t'tha diamond?"

Suddenly, the air became electric. A ball game on school time! Locking horns with the French and Italians in a baseball game was, in itself, high adventure, but cutting school to do it was double-barreled excitement. The prime factor was Clarence Hooker.

Clarence Hooker was our high school principal and a self-appointed sergeant-at-arms in matters of truancy and other infractions. At random times he would walk into the assembly hall and take a quick head count of the male population. If he came up too short, he'd jump in his car and cruise around to the favorite hang-outs, swooping down on any fugitives like an eagle on a rabbit. Hooker's idea of rehabilitation was straightforward: sudden and swift pain. Mutt Hukala had recently gotten into a discussion with Hooker regarding the civil rights of students caught smoking in the boy's toilet. With one lightning move, Hooker caught Mutt with a left jab to the nose, removed the pack of cigarettes from Mutt's shirt pocket, and had walked away before the first drop of blood had hit the floor. Clarence Hooker was nobody to fool around with.

La Farge stood there smirking, knowing full well that Mutt's nose remembered that incident. But the vernal juices, too long pent up by the months of winter, were flowing strong through Mutt's veins. He looked around at the Finn population. "OK, La Farge, you gotta game! Everybody go home an' get their gloves!"

Mutt looked at me. "You kin take five guys in yer car can't ya?"

"Wait a minute, Mutt. I don't think this is..."

"C'mon, c'mon! We don't have time to walk the three miles out to the diamond, an' yer not gonna back down from this salami squad are ya? Besides, yer our right fielder!"

I couldn't resist the peer pressure and the right-field honors, so I got my glove, went back to the station, and picked up five of our team.

The game was a resounding success with the Finns coming away with a 10 to 8 victory. Part of the credit had to be attributed to forethought on the part of Reino Rovaniemi, who brought a brand-new baseball to the game. What only a few of us knew was that it had been given a coat of Johnson's Car Wax, which effectively took away the bite on La Farge's curve ball. Smoky complained loudly about the feel of the ball when he first grabbed it, but we convinced him that he had just forgotten what a new ball felt like.

We were in a festive mood, driving back to town in the Widow-Maker, recounting highlights of the game as we approached the crest of Park City Hill, when an Oldsmobile passed us going in the opposite direction, and I locked eyes with the driver.

It was Clarence Hooker.

"Ohmigawd!!!! It's Hooker!"

Mutt, who was sitting next to me in the middle of the front seat, whipped his head around and looked out the rear window. "Gawdammit, it is! An' he's stopping an' turning around! Step on it!"

I looked at him in disbelief. "He looked right at me, an' he knows my car!"

"Yeah, stupid, but he don't know who's with you!" And with that he grabbed the steering column throttle with both hands and pushed it all the way down.

The Model A Ford had a very early form of cruise control with a throttle lever mounted on the steering column which overrode the gas petal on the floor. Mutt Hukala now had full control of the speed of the Widow-Maker.

The Widow-Maker's engine instantly underwent a personality change. The friendly bucketa-bucketa turned into a nasty snarl, and we started hurling precipitously down Park City Hill.

Park City was a tiny outcropping of houses south of town at the top of a mile-long hill on M-28, a narrow two-lane asphalt highway connecting US-41 and points south. In the spring, M-28 was always liberally laced with potholes.

I clawed at Mutt's hands holding the throttle. "Leggo, fer chrissake! You'll kill us!!"

"Hooker'll kill us if he catches us!"

Reino Rovaniemi, sitting next to Mutt by the right-hand door, looked out of his window. "Here he comes—he'll catch us sure as hell—that's a new car he's got!"

Steering had now become an all-consuming task, as I whipped the necker's knob back and forth furiously, trying to keep the Widow-Maker on the road and miss the largest of the potholes. I shot a glance over at the speedometer which was a graduated cylinder mounted behind a small glass window.

It was just passing sixty!

Christ! I had absolutely no idea how fast this car would go before it disintegrated.

My eyes got back on the road just as the right wheel met a gigantic pothole. At the same time, the fish line which was still holding up the right end of the front bumper gave up the ghost and the bumper hit the highway.

SSSCCCRRREEEEEEEEEEEE!!!!!!
CCCRRRRAAKK...CCCRRRRRUUUUNNNCCCCHHHHHH!!!!!

Just as on the night that I was driving to the Evergreen Drive-In, the steering wheel started to violently jerk to the right. However, at the speed we were now travelling, the torque on the bumper was so great that it instantly tore the left bracket bolt loose, and we ran over my own front bumper. As it passed under the car, it lashed up and shattered the floorboards underneath Reino's feet.

Reino jerked his feet up and looked down at the blurred roadway in horror, thinking that some subterranean monster had just tried to pluck him from the car. "Whatwazzatt...?"

"The front bumper!" I didn't have time for small talk.

Reino looked at me with bulging eyes. "Stop this thing... I wanna get out!"

Mutt shifted his grip on the hand throttle. "Ain't nobody gettin' out! Where's Hooker?"

Kippy Hanson, one of our Methodist free agents sitting in the back seat, looked out the rear window. "He hadda slow down to keep from hittin' yer bumper, but he's pickin' up speed again."

Mutt turned to me. "You say you've taken this heap through the Swedetown Puddle?"

"Yep."

"Well, let's do 'er again. Maybe Hooker's car'll stall out."

I looked at the gaping hole beneath Reino's feet. "Reino, yer not gonna like this one bit!"

The Widow-Maker was now making an eerie, whistling roar and was vibrating badly. I looked over at the speedometer, and all I saw was a white sightless eye where the numbers should have been. We had exceeded the design specifications of the car and were travelling in an uncharted realm.

As we approached the road to the Swedetown Puddle, I turned to Mutt. "If you don't leggo the throttle, we'll never make this turn."

Mutt took his hands from the throttle and I pushed it up, slamming on the brakes and whipping into the left turn at high speed. The Widow-Maker tilted precariously over on its right wheels, spewing gravel in all directions. The right door suddenly popped open, and Reino, who had been hanging onto it for dear life, swung out into space.

"EEEEIIIIIIIAAAAAAAAHHHHHHHH!!!!!"

Mutt quickly grabbed him by the back of his belt and yanked him back into the car.

Reino was now shaking very badly. "Lemme out!!! Lemme out!!"

Mutt elbowed him viciously in the ribs. "Shaddup! You almos' gotcher wish!"

We hit the Swedetown Puddle, and the inside of the car exploded with water, mud, and steam. Reino gave out another hideous scream as he bore the full brunt of the barrage. I tore off my cap and swabbed the inside of the windshield. Again, the Widow-Maker sailed right through without so much as a hiccup.

The three of us in the front seat now resembled mud creatures from outer space. Mutt turned to Hanson in the back seat. "Where's Hooker—did he make it through the puddle?"

"That really slowed him down, but he's pulling out of it right now. Hey, there's a wheel following us!...chrisssakes! It's one of ours!"

I looked up in rear view mirror, but couldn't see a thing because of the vibration.

Mutt craned his head around. "Yup. You've lost one of the right wheels, I think. If you slow down now, she's gonna come right down on the drum."

Hanson yelled from the back seat, "Hooker almos' hit yer tire! He mus' think we're rippin' stuff off the car an'throwin' em at him!"

Mutt thought for a few seconds. "Look. Go out that road by Keskitalo's house. There's a gravel-covered fill right next to the cedar swamp. We'll ditch the car on the fill an' spread out in the swamp."

I followed his directions, while making sure that the Widow-maker kept going fast enough to stay up on three wheels. We came up to the gravel fill and turned into it without slackening speed. I slammed on the brakes and gritted my teeth.

The Widow-Maker sideslipped across the gravel, throwing rocks in all directions and lurching drunkenly to the right as it came down on the rear wheel drum. In a massive cloud of gravel, mud, water, steam, and sparks we ground to a halt, like a Flying Fortress making a wheels-up forced landing.

The six of us boiled out of the car and scattered like partridge into the swamp. Mutt and I stayed together, and after we got about a hundred yards in, stopped, squatted down, and watched the car. It sat there in a pathetic heap on three wheels, covered with mud, steam hissing from the radiator. My once-proud mistress, now an object of despair.

Hooker pulled up a few moments later. He pawed around in the inside of the Widow-Maker, looking for clues to the identity of the other occupants, glancing up occasionally to glare off into the swamp.

I was starting to become aware of my surroundings: squatting in icy water with my legs turning numb. I looked over at Mutt. "This was a great idea, Mutt, heading out into this swamp just after the ice has melted."

Mutt pulled out a can of Copenhagen snuff from his shirt pocket and tucked a pinch under his lower lip. "Quitcher bitchin'. Yer alive, ain'tcha? I'll say one thing, though. That's one helluva car you got."

The following March, I was sitting in the assembly hall one gray Monday morning trying to plumb the mysteries of solid geometry when a heavy hand clamped on my shoulder. I looked up at Clarence Hooker.

"You gotta minute?"

"Yessir."

I followed him into the hallway. He turned to me and pushed his iron-rimmed spectacles up the bridge of his nose.

"I see where you've gotten accepted at the University of Michigan for next fall."

"Uh...yessir, that's right."

"Well, you've gotta good head on your shoulders, when somebody isn't talking you into doing something stupid."

Hooker had unerringly named all eighteen of us in front of the assembly the Monday following the Widow-Maker's run. He had dealt out reprisals in the form of having us refurbish the school wood shop after school for four weeks. For Hooker, this was mild punishment indeed.

The Widow-Maker had gotten pieced back together after a period of time at Chub's Standard station. It had achieved a certain degree of notoriety, and underclassmen who had been victims of Hooker's truancy sweeps would come over to the station and look at it in awe. Even Alice Maki had taken to boasting how we had brought the Packard to its knees at the Evergreen Drive-In.

Hooker continued the conversation. "They've got rules down there. They're not gonna let you drive the Widow-Maker on campus."

"Uh...yessir, I guess that's right."

"Well, when you leave in the fall, I want to buy 'er."

"The Widow-Maker?"

"That's right. You paid Arne Setala ninety dollars for it, right?"

"Well, that's right, but..."

"I'll give you the same price for it. Cars depreciate, you know, so that's more than generous." He stepped in a little closer and bared his false teeth just a fraction. "Isn't it?"

"Oh yessir!!! More than generous!"

"That car's got a reputation now, and the last damn thing I need is to be chasing it around the countryside with some other idiot at the wheel. If that car stays around here, I'm gonna be the one who's driving it! Is that clear?"

"Yessir! Very clear! But you ought'a know that there's things wrong with it. The battery's just about shot, the right rear tire keeps leaking air..."

"That's OK, I'll take care of 'em later. We'll close the deal in September!" He stalked off down the hallway.

Nobody could ever accuse me of giving them the hard sell.